T0328651

Cambridge Elements

Elements in Child Development
edited by
Marc H. Bornstein
Eunice Kennedy Shriver National Institute of Child Health and Human Development, Bethesda
Institute for Fiscal Studies, London
UNICEF, New York City

CHILDREN'S IMAGINATION

Paul L. Harris
Harvard University, Graduate School of Education

CAMBRIDGE
UNIVERSITY PRESS

CAMBRIDGE
UNIVERSITY PRESS

University Printing House, Cambridge CB2 8BS, United Kingdom

One Liberty Plaza, 20th Floor, New York, NY 10006, USA

477 Williamstown Road, Port Melbourne, VIC 3207, Australia

314–321, 3rd Floor, Plot 3, Splendor Forum, Jasola District Centre, New Delhi – 110025, India

103 Penang Road, #05–06/07, Visioncrest Commercial, Singapore 238467

Cambridge University Press is part of the University of Cambridge.

It furthers the University's mission by disseminating knowledge in the pursuit of education, learning, and research at the highest international levels of excellence.

www.cambridge.org
Information on this title: www.cambridge.org/9781009066037
DOI: 10.1017/9781009067423

First published 2022

A catalogue record for this publication is available from the British Library.

ISBN 978-1-009-06603-7 Paperback
ISSN 2632-9948 (online)
ISSN 2632-993X (print)

Children's Imagination

Elements in Child Development

DOI: 10.1017/9781009067423
First published online: June 2022

Paul L. Harris
Harvard University, Graduate School of Education
Author for correspondence: Paul L. Harris, paul_harris@gse.harvard.edu

Abstract: Children's imagination was traditionally seen as a wayward, desire-driven faculty that is eventually constrained by rationality. A more recent, Romantic view claims that young children's fertile imagination is increasingly dulled by schooling. Contrary to both perspectives, this Element argues that, paradoxically, children's imagination draws much inspiration from reality. Hence, when they engage in pretend play, envision the future, or conjure up counterfactual possibilities, children rarely generate fantastical possibilities. Their reality-guided imagination enables children to plan ahead and to engage in informative thought experiments. Nevertheless, when adults present children with less reality-based possibilities – via biblical narratives or the endorsement of special beings – they are receptive. Indeed, such imaginary possibilities can infuse their otherwise commonsensical appraisal of reality. Finally, like adults, young children enjoy being absorbed into a make-believe, fictional world, but faced with real-world problems calling for creativity, they often need guidance, given their limited knowledge of prior solutions.

Keywords: imagination, pretend, future planning, counterfactual thinking, absorption

ISBNs: 9781009066037 (PB), 9781009067423 (OC)
ISSNs: 2632-9948 (online), 2632-993X (print)

Contents

1 The Nature of the Imagination

Definitions of the imagination often have a normative component. Idle thoughts about the not here and the not now, the kinds of fleeting thoughts that occur to us when daydreaming, are not generally seen as worthy products of the imagination. Only richer, more active, and creative fantasies are seen as genuinely imaginative. However, because I want to trace the imagination from its origins in early childhood, I propose to be more inclusive – to suppress any urge to exclude transient or pedestrian episodes of make-believe in favor of creative or sustained flights of fantasy. As we will see, this inclusive strategy is helpful because it encourages an analysis of overlooked but important aspects of the imagination.

Definitions of the imagination are also likely to imply an engagement with unrealized possibilities rather than known actualities. However, consider what happens when children listen to a historical narrative. Provided the narrative is an accurate account, the events described, whether in the time of the Romans, the Vikings, or the Civil War, have actually happened. Yet children listening to that narrative cannot draw on any memory of the events in question. To follow the narrative, they need to construct their own mental representation of what took place, and that constructive process can reasonably be called an act of the imagination. More generally, this example underlines the fact that children, and adults too, deploy their imagination not only when they conjure up fantastical possibilities that may never be realized but also when they are told about actual events that have already taken place. By implication, an inclusive strategy is helpful because it invites us to think about an aspect of the imagination that is pervasive but neglected, notably our ability to contemplate in our mind's eye not just fictional or made-up events but also real events that we have not actually observed. Vygotsky made this important but neglected point almost a century ago: "When we read a newspaper and find out about a thousand events that we have not directly witnessed, when a child studies geography or history, when we merely learn what has been happening to another person by reading a letter from him – in all these cases our imagination serves our experience" (Vygotsky, 2004, p. 17).

In summary, I will argue that an act of the imagination takes place when children think about events or entities that are not observably present. Such events or entities may have already happened, they may be imminent but as yet unrealized, or they may be fantastical and unlikely to ever materialize. What unites them as targets of the imagination is that the child contemplating them is not simply drawing on direct perception or retrieving the memory of an earlier encounter but is constructing a novel representation. Admittedly, that constructive process can and often does draw heavily on memory. For example, what children envisage about historical or future events is likely to draw on their memory of the past, but still there is an important conceptual difference between the simple retrieval of an event that one actually observed and imagining an event that one never witnessed, even if children sometimes have difficulty in discriminating the one from the other, as discussed in Section 6.

Although I will not strive to make a sharp distinction between allegedly creative and more humdrum acts of the imagination, I will have frequent recourse to a related distinction. Sometimes, children are in the driver's seat: when they engage in pretend play with props, create an imaginary friend, or invent a story, it is they who are taking the initiative in generating the imaginary materials. By contrast, when they are told about the Tooth Fairy or listen to a narrative from a history book or from the Bible, the target of their imagination has been specified externally by a parent, a teacher, or a text. As we will see, what children are prone to generate for themselves is likely to be different from what they contemplate in their imagination with external support. In particular, the latter will often be more fantastical and reality defying. That said, and despite the validity of this distinction, the imaginary entities that children first hear about in a story, or see on a screen, may eventually come to inspire their own imaginative activities down the road. The child who is presented with stories about rabbits in the garden is likely to generate a different imaginary world from the child who is presented with cartoons about superheroes in outer space.

In the sections that follow, I organize the materials with an eye to development. I start by describing one of the very earliest manifestations of the imagination – already evident among toddlers – notably the emergence of pretend play with props (Section 2) as well as early role-play (Section 3). I then go on to describe capacities that emerge in early childhood: the ability to imagine what the future might bring (Section 4) as well as the ability to imagine possibilities that could have happened – but never actually came to pass (Section 5). I then discuss how far children's imagination infuses their claims about what actually happened (Section 6). Granted the importance of stories in children's lives, I review the ways in which children process narratives, become absorbed in the worlds that they describe, and sometimes construct their own imaginary or fictional worlds (Section 7). Finally, I review children's inventiveness, focusing on two central human skills – the ability to invent and make tools and the ability to draw (Section 8). In Section 9, I review the main themes of this Element.

2 Pretend Play

Most typically developing children have started to engage in pretend play by the time they pass their second birthday. For example, they pretend to feed a doll by holding a cup to its lips, give it a pretend bath in a cardboard box, or with the help of suitable props, act out some workaday activity, such as cleaning or cooking. The emergence of this type of playful reenactment of familiar routines seems to be unique to human children. Admittedly, there have been anecdotal accounts of very occasional, prop-based pretending by chimpanzees, both domesticated and wild (Suddendorf & Whiten, 2001), but among young, non-human primates, there is no evidence for the systematic, pretend reenactment of familiar routines that is seen so regularly in human toddlers.

2.1 Pretending across Cultures

Pretend play emerges across a wide range of cultures and does not seem to depend on systematic support or instruction from adults (Callaghan et al., 2011; Harris & Jalloul, 2013). In some cultures, adults are prone to offer toys as props or join in with children's pretend play, but in other cultures they provide little scaffolding (Bornstein, 2007; Gaskins, 2000). Yet, in either case, we see approximately the same capacity for pretend play emerging. By implication, pretend play reflects a universal, species-specific disposition to imagine activities and events that are not actually taking place but can be represented with the help of suitable actions and props. One might be tempted to conclude that such pretend play is simply a reflection of children's capacity for relatively accurate imitation (Harris, 2012, chapter 3). Perhaps, children watch a parent cooking or digging and reproduce those actions as best as they can with whatever props are to hand. However, key aspects of pretend play involve more than simple imitation. The child playing with a doll likely conjures up, in their imagination, the juice in the proffered cup or the water in the prepared bath.

Strong evidence for such imaginative interpolations comes from collaborative pretend play. In the course of the third year, toddlers not only produce prop-based, pretend play themselves, they can also join in with a play partner and make sense of what they are up to (Harris & Kavanaugh, 1993). For example, if they see a partner pick up an empty teapot and mischievously "pour" pretend tea over a toy animal, they realize what will have happened as a result. They appropriately describe the animal victim as "wet" and "dry" it with a tissue. It is easy to underestimate the thinking that is required to make this type of collaborative engagement possible, but a moment's reflection reveals the complexity of what is going on. When the partner lifts the empty teapot and tilts it in a pretend pouring gesture, no liquid actually comes out.

So, to describe the animal victim as "wet" or to subsequently "dry" it, the child needs to imagine liquid coming out of the teapot spout and dousing the animal underneath. In that sense, the child's participation goes well beyond simple imitation. To engage in the relevant acts of the imagination, tailored to a partner's initiatives, the child must be guided or constrained by real-world knowledge, such as the fact that teapots typically contain liquid, that a liquid will emerge if it is tilted, that liquids fall downward rather than upward or sideways, and so forth. Indeed, although it is tempting to think that children's pretend play is fanciful and allows them to escape from humdrum reality, it is routinely guided by their knowledge of the way that everyday reality works (Harris, 2021).

In fact, evidence for "escapist" pretend play in which children conjure up an exotic alternative to the real world is sparse. Young children mostly recreate the everyday world that they themselves are familiar with – its scripts and regularities. They reenact domestic routines such as eating, drinking, cooking, and cleaning rather than visits to the moon or the ocean floor. Research in traditional cultures underlines how children are keen observers of the everyday activities they see around them. Particularly in cultures where children have plenty of opportunities to watch adults at work, they are likely to engage in "work-themed" pretense: pretend reenactments of the kinds of tasks they see nearby adults engaged in. Indeed, in a study of play among Ngandu subsistence farmers and Aka foragers in the Central African Republic, Boyette (2016) found that the pretend reenactment of subsistence activities, such as pretending to cook inedible leaves or fetching make-believe water in small containers, was the dominant mode of pretend play in each setting.

Lew-Levy et al. (2020) offered additional evidence for such workaday pretense in two hunter-gatherer groups: Tanzanian Hazda and Congolese BaYaka. Sustained observation of individual children (ranging from three to eighteen years) confirmed that play took up a considerable proportion of their daily time budgets: between a fifth and a quarter. Moreover, a good deal of their playtime was devoted to pretend play: 41 percent among the Hazda and 31 percent among the BaYaka. Echoing the findings of Boyette (2016), pretend play was dominated by workaday themes such as playing house, play hunting, play foraging, or doll play. Moreover, reflecting the division of labor in the adult community, girls in both communities spent more time than boys in pretend housekeeping, whereas boys spent more time than girls in pretend hunting. Pretend play that did not reflect work themes (e.g., pretending to sleep, pretending to ride in cars, pretending to be animals, imitating adult social interaction, or imitating religious ceremonies) did occur, but it was considerably less frequent than work-themed pretense.

A study conducted with five different cultural groups in Brazil reported similar results (Gosso et al., 2007). The themes that children enacted were mainly drawn from everyday life; very few (<5 percent) involved fantasy. Moreover, when the characters that children invented or enacted were analyzed, the majority (approaching 90 percent) was based on real people or animals; few were fantastic characters such as a vampire.

2.2 Pretending in Preschool

Early childhood educators have long been interested in the possibility that pretend play, especially social pretend play, might provide a cognitive boost for young children. This interest is both theoretical and practical. From a theoretical perspective, Vygotsky (1978) claimed that when engaged in pretend play, young children are induced to be well regulated in the sense that they strive to honor the rules and roles of the make-believe scenario that they are enacting. Arguably then, frequent pretend play would lead to improvements in self-control, as indexed by measures of executive function.

From a practical perspective, encouraging young children to engage in pretend is a relatively easy task. They can be prompted with themes and props. Indeed, well-designed intervention studies have shown that when adults offer support, especially via a combination of play materials (e.g., firefighters' helmets, a medical kit), verbal prompting (e.g., "Let's play firefighters"), and modeling, preschoolers are likely to engage in higher-quality pretend play than they do without such support. They are more likely to act continuously in roles (e.g., as a firefighter or doctor), to communicate their play plans, and to engage in connected episodes of pretense (Kalkusch et al., 2021).

If such simple interventions aimed at boosting social pretend play were to have notable cognitive benefits, that would be welcome news because they can be easily introduced into a range of classroom settings at low cost. However, much of the evidence indicating that pretend play delivers cognitive benefits is suggestive rather than solid, given a variety of design issues (Lillard et al., 2013). I describe some recent exemplary studies that continue to offer tantalizing rather than robust evidence for the benefits of pretend play interventions.

White et al. (2021) observed Spanish-speaking preschoolers in their classrooms over a year-long period. Children were scored for the frequency with which they engaged in social pretense in concert with other children as well as solitary pretense. Children's performance on the day-night task, a well-established measure of executive function, was assessed twice, once in the fall and once in the following spring, making it possible to determine what factors predicted the degree to which children's scores improved. The extent to which children had engaged in social pretense proved to be a helpful predictor of improvement, whereas the degree to which they had engaged in solitary pretense did not. Children's involvement in nonpretense social play was also unrelated to improvement on the executive function measure. By implication, there was something about the combination of (i) playing with other children and (ii) engaging in pretense that was a predictor of executive function gain, and it is tempting to infer that this combination was causally responsible for improvements in executive function. However, as usual, it is risky to draw causal conclusions from correlational data. After all, it is possible that some third factor, for example, being attentive to rapidly changing cues, facilitated children's participation in the back and forth of social pretense as well as their performance on the day-night task.

More persuasive evidence of a causal impact of pretend play on self-control or executive function could be provided by controlled intervention studies in which some children but not others are prompted to engage in pretend play, especially social pretend play with a social component. In one study of this type, Thibodeau et al. (2016) looked at the impact of an intervention with four-year-olds from predominantly middle-income families. Teachers worked with small groups of children for a total of just over six hours spread over a five-week period, encouraging them to engage in (i) pretend play, (ii) nonpretend activities such as coloring or ball games, or (iii) normal classroom activities. In anticipation of improvements in executive function, children were assessed before and after the intervention on three different aspects of executive function. None of the three groups displayed any significant improvement on a measure of attention shifting or on the day-night task. However, children in the pretend play group, unlike children in the other two groups, showed a modest gain on a measure of working memory, as indexed by digit span. Moreover, that gain was more evident among those children in the pretend play group who consistently engaged in more exotic pretending (e.g., pretending to be a fairy) as compared with more prosaic pretending (e.g., pretending to be a mom). By implication, the discipline of enacting a less familiar and more demanding scenario was especially likely to boost concentration and memory, as indexed by the digit span task. That said, this difference emerged only in a post hoc analysis of individual differences; the pretend play intervention straddled both exotic and prosaic scenarios so that we do not have experimental evidence for the difference between the two types of pretense.

In another intervention study, Goldstein and Lerner (2018) compared three groups of four- to five-year-olds from low-income families. Guided by an adult, one group engaged in sociodramatic pretend play, a second engaged in construction play with blocks, and a third listened to stories and answered questions about them. All three groups received three 20-minute intervention sessions per week for a total of eight weeks (i.e., eight hours in total). Before and after the intervention, children received various tests of socioemotional development (theory-of-mind understanding, sharing stickers with another child, comforting an adult in pain, negative reactions to an adult's pain, spontaneously helping an adult in evident need of practical assistance, and verbal reports of empathic reactions to another's distress). Intervention effects were found for two of these six measures. As compared with children in the other two control groups, children in the pretend play group showed fewer negative reactions to an adult's pain and reported less empathic reactions to another's distress.

Summarizing across these two intervention studies, it remains unclear exactly what effects such interventions can have. Despite relatively sustained and high dosages of pretend play (i.e., a total of six to eight hours across several weeks), the effects in each study were limited rather than pervasive. They emerged for only one of the three executive function measures in the study by Thibodeau et al. (2016) and for only two of the six socioemotional measures in the study by Goldstein and Lerner (2018). Moreover, current theorizing provides no straightforward explanation of why some effects were found whereas others were not. For example, it is not clear why the pretend play intervention *reduced* children's empathic reactions to another's distress – even if post hoc explanations might be offered. Finally, it is worth remembering that millions of children grow up in traditional cultures without the alleged benefits of adult-guided pretend play – they are often left to their own devices or left with older children who are likely to scaffold the pretend play of younger children. What to conclude then about such intervention research? My own recommendation would be to switch to less lengthy and more targeted experimental studies in which the primary goal is to pinpoint and analyze the complicated processes that underlie pretend play. Once that goal is achieved, we may be better placed to seek and demonstrate the potential educational benefits of large-scale, sustained pretend play interventions. I describe examples of such targeted experimental studies in the context of role-play – as discussed Section 3.

2.3 Conclusions

Most typically developing children have started to engage in pretend play by their second birthday, often doing so with minimal guidance or prompting from caregivers. When children engage in pretend play, they readily draw on and interpolate their knowledge of everyday causal regularities, especially when making sense of a partner's pretend enactments. For example, they imagine the pouring or drinking of a pretend liquid. In that sense, early pretend play goes beyond simple imitation. Nevertheless, in choosing pretend themes, young children often draw on their observation of the adult activities they have seen, frequently engaging in work-themed pretense. In both these respects, children's pretend play is inspired by their observation and grasp of everyday reality. More fantastical creations and enactments are rare.

Research in early childhood education often aims to show the cognitive benefits of play, especially pretend play. Although observational research points to such benefits, we lack cumulative evidence from successful, well-designed interventions.

3 Role-Play

In one important respect, children clearly defy reality in the course of their pretend play. They often set their own identity aside and imagine what it would be like to be someone else. Such role-play or perspective-taking comes in a variety of forms, but these forms can be distilled into three basic types depending on the particular pretend vehicle that children deploy. First, children sometimes impersonate or act as if they themselves were another person or an animal. For example, they might temporarily, and sometimes recurrently, pretend to be a dog, a mother, or a train driver. Second, children sometimes invest a prop, typically, although not always, a doll or toy, with person-like qualities, for example a name or at least a distinctive identity and characteristics. Third, children can conjure up, out of thin air, so to speak, another person or creature and engage with them, as if they were actually present, despite their evident invisibility (Harris, 2000).

Across these different vehicles for their imagination – the self, a prop, or nothing at all – children, from their second birthday upward, typically endow the particular being that they imagine with various psychological properties – thoughts, feelings, preferences, perceptions, knowledge, all of which provide a basis for having an interpersonal connection to the being in question. Many of these role-playing episodes are fleeting. For example, the child animates a lifeless doll, a stuffed animal, or a toy giraffe with the capacities and needs appropriate to a particular episode of pretend play, such as hunger or thirst, fear or anger, feeling too hot or too cold, or a need to be cuddled. These pretend attributions do not outlive the make-believe episode that is being enacted. Sometimes, however, and increasingly in the course of the preschool years, children invoke a particular imaginary being on a regular basis, repeatedly attributing to him, her, or it the same name, identity, and characteristics. At this point, we are witnessing the emergence of what is commonly known as an imaginary companion.

For more than a century, psychologists have gone back and forth about the definition, scope, and ubiquity of this intriguing aspect of the child's imagination. My own preference is (again) to be inclusive rather than exclusive. For example, even if the phenomenon looks very different to an external observer depending on the particular vehicle that a child deploys to enact the pretense (i.e., whether it is the self, a doll, or a purely imaginary being conjured out of nothing at all), it is plausible, from the child's own perspective, and indeed in terms of the underlying mechanism, that these various forms of pretend play belong to the same psychological family. After all, they all involve a specific act of the imagination, notably the creation of an imaginary being endowed with psychological attributes. Similarly, although from the observer's perspective, the child who engages in transient role-play with a doll may look very different from the child who insists on the existence of a totally invisible companion for months on end, it is unlikely that there is a fundamental psychological discontinuity between the two. In both instances, the child is imagining the existence, agency, and perspective of another being, someone different from the self. The only difference is one of temporal span or, more precisely, the degree to which the child reverts repeatedly in their imagination to the same persona.

Indeed, Vostrovsky (1895), who was the first psychologist to call attention to the fact that some pretend beings become "a part of the environment of the child for a greater length of time – sometimes for years," made the equally important observation that children also conjure up make-believe persons in a transient fashion. In the context of pretend play, they readily populate a pretend house, school, or bus with the appropriate occupants.

In summary, my proposal is that young children have a natural disposition to pretend to be someone they are not. Whether they do so briefly or repeatedly, with the help of a prop or without, the basic psychological maneuver is similar, namely, to imagine the world from the perspective of that other being. That said, there are changes in the kinds of attributions that toddlers make, with younger toddlers prone to treat the other as a sentient but passive recipient of their ministrations and older children more likely to endow the other with independent agency and increasingly with a range of mental states, including sensations, feelings, thoughts, and plans (Wolf et al., 1984).

3.1 The Frequency of Imaginary Companions

With these definitional issues laid out, it is worth providing some facts and figures about the frequency of imaginary companions as conventionally defined (i.e., those companions that persist over weeks or months). The work of Taylor et al. (2004) is especially helpful in this regard. Two notable conclusions have emerged from her sustained research program. First, particularly if we adopt a relatively inclusive definition, the creation of an imaginary companion is not confined to a handful of especially imaginative children. Among US children, approximately two-thirds have at least one imaginary companion – and sometimes more – at some point in early childhood (i.e., from approximately three to eight years of age), whereas the remaining children never create one throughout that same period. It turns out that having an imaginary companion in the course of early childhood is not so exceptional.

Is the creation of such an enduring companion connected to a particular personality type or ability? First, we may say, fairly unequivocally, in light of the research by Taylor and her colleagues, that there is no evidence that their creation indexes an emotional disturbance or pathology. The very prevalence of their creation – by all sorts of children – speaks against any such connection. However, there is some evidence, tantalizing rather than completely solid, that children with imaginary companions are somewhat better at "mentalizing," that is, better at thinking about and identifying mental states (Harris, 2005). Such a connection is not implausible – after all, as we have seen, the creation of an imaginary companion typically calls for an ability to think about and attribute mental states to that companion.

3.2 Encouraging Role-Play

Given the possible connection between having an imaginary companion and mentalizing, it is tempting to think that prompting children to engage in more role-play, or more elaborate role-play, could benefit their social cognition and increase their insight into mental states. Indeed, a responsive adult armed with ideas and props can help children to explore pretend scenarios that they might not have generated for themselves. For example, in a longitudinal study, Slade (1987) filmed children from twenty to twenty-eight months as they played with various toys and props. The length of pretend bouts and their sophistication were greater when mothers were available as play partners rather than physically present but engaged in conversation with the experimenter. Moreover, mothers were especially likely to boost their child's pretend if they actively participated in the pretend episodes themselves rather than simply offering a verbal commentary.

Similarly, when preschool teachers encouraged pretend role-play by suggesting themes and providing props, young children's pretend play was richer than it would ordinarily be (Kalkusch et al., 2021). Once that external support was withdrawn, however, children displayed little evidence of any longer-term benefit from the intervention (Perren et al., 2021). They may well have enjoyed the enriched curriculum, but that does not mean that their subsequent imaginative role-play grew richer or stronger as a result. A plausible assessment of these negative findings is that, actually, they are not so negative. More specifically, as argued earlier, the tendency to engage in role-play, whether fleeting or sustained, is natural and robust in most children. Interventions by adults might prompt particular manifestations of that natural tendency – for example, playing nurse or firefighter depending on the suggestions and props that adults supply – but we have no persuasive evidence that they have a stable impact on the strength of the natural tendency itself.

Nevertheless, if most children can readily engage in role-play, it is clearly worth asking whether more localized and targeted interventions can enable children to put that preexisting ability to use in order to achieve a discrete cognitive or emotional objective. Earlier, I suggested that children's role-play involves a temporary setting aside of the self. Children imagine what it would be like to be another person or another creature. But when stated in this bald fashion, it is tempting to be skeptical. Is it really feasible that young children, notoriously egocentric in their thinking, are capable of such self-abnegation? Apparently, yes! In a series of studies, Carlson and her colleagues invited young children to pretend to be someone other than themselves and then looked for repercussions on the way that they subsequently behaved. For example, in one study, three- and four-year-olds were invited to pretend that they were Batman or Dora the Explorer (White & Carlson, 2016). To help them initiate and sustain this role-playing pretense, children were given suitable props (such as a cape or backpack). Then they were invited to perform a challenging, executive function task that called for them to sort cards accurately based on a succession of shifting rules (e.g., sorting cards by shape vs. sorting by color). The key finding was that, although role-playing instructions had no impact on three-year-olds, five-year-old role-players outperformed a control group of non-role-players, who had been given no specific instructions or, alternatively, prompted to simply remain themselves and reflect on their own thoughts (e.g., "I want you to ask yourself, 'Where do *I* think this card should go'?").

In a follow-up study, four- and six-year-olds were asked to be a "good helper" by working at a relatively boring computer-based task in which, on a succession of trials, they had to press the space bar if a particular target stimulus appeared but not press any key if another, nontarget stimulus appeared (White et al., 2017). As a respite from this wearisome task children could, if they wished, take a break and play an iPad game. The iPad was placed – invitingly – beside them. Not surprisingly, children preferred the iPad game. Over a ten-minute period, they spent around three and half minutes being a good helper on the boring task and spent the rest of the time on the iPad, although six-year-olds were in general better helpers than four-year-olds. However, in both age groups, children's time allocation shifted depending on the role-playing instructions they had received. Children who were pretending to be someone else, such as Batman or Dora the Explorer, spent more time being good helpers and were less susceptible to the temptations of the iPad than children prompted to remain themselves.

The intriguing implication of these two studies is that, temporarily at least, preschoolers can set their own self aside and pretend to be someone else, reaping benefits in terms of both concentration and persistence. Less clear is the mechanism involved. One possibility is that role-play is effective because the preoccupations and priorities of the self are temporarily put on hold such that disruptions to concentration and persistence are minimized. A different possibility is that role-play is effective because it can provide an aspirational boost – while temporarily in the shoes of Batman or Dora, children feel more mature and aim to be more cooperative than their actual selves. Still, it is worth noting that the benefits of prompted role-play are not ubiquitous – when children were given a challenging task, namely, to retrieve a toy from inside a transparent box by opening it with the right key from a set of keys (none of which actually worked), role-play had no impact on children's persistence (Grenell et al., 2019). Although six-year-olds spent more time trying to open the box than four-year-olds, persistence was not boosted by role-play. A plausible implication is that role-play might help children to persist on a relatively tedious task that they would not ordinarily choose to engage in – one that calls for concentration and flexibility in responding to a shifting stimulus array – but has little discernible impact if children are already autonomously invested in a task, such as seeking to extract a toy.

3.3 Conclusions

Role-play is one of the most remarkable aspects of early pretend play. Although some children use their capacity for role-play to create relatively enduring companions, the frequency of such creations implies that the children who create them may not be a special group with distinctive abilities but rather one portion of a normally distributed disposition to engage in role-play, a disposition ranging from the fleeting and intermittent to the stable and persistent. If this analysis is correct, it would imply that research exploring the benefits of short-term role-play, tailored to the exigencies of particular environments and particular social situations, is likely to be fruitful, insofar as most young children are capable of it.

4 Thinking about Possibilities

We do not know for certain what the future holds, but, to varying degrees, we can anticipate what is likely to happen. Whether with respect to our own selves, or the future of our community, we can be either bold or cautious. But no matter how far we are inclined, temperamentally, toward sanguine or pessimistic expectations, our thoughts about the future involve an element of uncertainty. Of course, there are certain aspects of the future that are eminently predictable: day follows night, spring follows winter, adulthood follows childhood – but setting these calendrical certainties aside, we, whether as individual agents or as members of a community, have some latitude in what we imagine will be happening weeks or years hence.

Despite that latitude, work with adults has revealed a surprisingly intimate relation between remembering the past and imagining the future. More specifically, for better or worse, we adults mine our memory for the past to help envisage what the future holds. Admittedly, this is a flawed strategy because the unprecedented can also happen. Still, it is a reasonable heuristic most of the time. Its routine benefits are highlighted by patients with long-term memory disorders. Such patients have problems in envisaging what will happen in the future, just as one would expect if memory of the past is used as a guide to the future (Hassabis et al., 2007). These findings have straightforward developmental implications. Unsurprisingly, children's memory of the past improves as they get older. Their narratives about the past become richer and more coherent. Granted the findings with adults, we can also expect that children's ability to imagine what will happen in the future also improves with age, consonant with their richer memories of the past, and indeed there is evidence for such an improvement with age. In addition, children in a given age group vary in the extent to which they can remember the past in a rich and detailed fashion, and such individual variation in memory for the past correlates positively with children's ability to envisage the future (Busby & Suddendorf, 2005; Hayne et al., 2011).

The ability to imagine what is going to happen, or is likely to happen, has an important practical payoff. It becomes feasible to plan appropriately for what is likely to happen. As might be expected, older children are better than younger children at such future planning. For example, when they learn that they will revisit a particular location in the future, older children are better at figuring out what items they should take with them for that upcoming visit (Atance, 2015). Moreover, in line with the findings showing that memories of the past and thoughts about the future are often linked, children plan better if they are alerted to those connecting links. Chernyak et al. (2017) invited preschoolers to talk about events from different time points. In subsequent testing, children proved to be more planful if they had talked either about the near past or the near future. The authors concluded that such conversations were helpful because they led children to think about their extended self across time, especially the links between the near past and the near future.

4.1 Thinking about What Can Happen

When children are invited to think not about whether something *will* happen but about whether or not something *can* happen, what do they say? Intuitively, we might expect two very different outcomes. On the one hand, children might be very conservative. After all, their experience of life is ordinarily very limited compared to that of an adult. If they consult their past experience, they might assume that very little could possibly happen beyond what they have already witnessed in the past. On the other hand, if, based on their imagination, children conjure up all sorts of fantastical possibilities – magical transformations and transpositions, giants, mermaids, superheroes, and so forth – then maybe they are open to all sorts of eventualities, including those that they have never witnessed but have no good reason to rule out.

As we will see, neither of these extremes captures the full developmental picture. Children are neither radical conservatives nor completely open-minded in judging what can happen. Indeed, their thinking changes in the course of development. They start off being relatively conservative but as they get older they become more open-minded. This greater flexibility occurs for two different reasons. First, children increasingly realize that remote or unusual possibilities cannot be completely ruled out. They come to understand that just because something is improbable and not something that they have experienced in the past, that does not mean it cannot happen. In this respect, children gradually become less bounded by their own restricted experience (Shtulman & Carey, 2007).

A second shift is more dependent on the particular culture in which children grow up. Children encounter a variety of narratives. Some are presented as true stories about historical events that actually happened; some are presented as pieces of fiction – fairy tales about events that defy everyday causality. Alongside these two narrative genres, the historical and the fantastical, children who grow up in a Christian or Muslim family are also likely to hear stories from the Bible or the Koran. Such stories can be paradoxical because they are typically presented to children as recounting events that actually took place and yet they often recount events that defy ordinary causality – children will be told about the parting of the seas, the transformation of water into wine, and so forth. As we will see, children who have received a religious education are likely to accept that such miracles are possible. In this respect, then, we again see a shift away from conservatism toward a larger conception of what is possible. For better or worse, religious instruction teaches children to accept that the ordinary impossible – a virgin birth, resurrection from the dead – can occur via divine intervention.

With this brief preview in place, I present evidence for four conclusions: first, generally speaking, young children are skeptical about magical or supernatural possibilities; second, their initially cautious or skeptical stance is refined as they increasingly differentiate between downright impossible outcomes and unusual but possible outcomes; third, religious instruction encourages children to believe that not just the unusual, but also the impossible, can be brought about by divine intervention; finally, by engaging in thought experiments, young children can better understand what can and cannot happen.

4.2 Children's Skepticism about Magic

In his early theorizing, Piaget claimed that children had little understanding of natural causality and were open to a variety of magical possibilities (Harris, 2009; Piaget, 1928). Provoked by Piaget's claims, Margaret Mead tested them among the children of Manus, one of the Admiralty Islands in the South Pacific (Mead, 1932). In principle, Manus children were a congenial sample for testing Piaget's ideas because, among adult Manus, beliefs in witchcraft and supernatural powers were rife. Accordingly, it was plausible to expect that the children would hold similar beliefs. However, when Mead invited them to explain a variety of untoward or malign outcomes, children offered only plausible, naturalistic explanations. For example, invited to say why a canoe might have gone adrift overnight, children did not think to invoke a malevolent witch but rather the fact that the canoe had not been properly moored in the first place. Mead concluded that young children were quite commonsensical in their everyday thinking about causality. Turning Piaget's ideas upside down, she argued that credence in the supernatural does not come naturally to children but is a belief system they gradually accept following participation and induction into the adult world.

Doubts about Piaget's claims were also reported by Huang (1930). Working with children in the United States, he showed them a variety of nonmagical but unusual or "strange" phenomena and asked children to explain how they came about. For example, he filled a tube with water, placed a piece of paper over the mouth of the tube, and inverted it. Children were puzzled by the fact that the card remained in place and appeared to stop the water from pouring out.

However, in trying to explain it, they typically invoked plausible (albeit incorrect) naturalistic explanations (e.g., "Perhaps the card sticks to the tube because it's wet.") rather than magical possibilities. In a subsequent review of a variety of post-Piagetian studies, Huang (1943) reinforced Mead's conclusion that children typically invoke naturalistic rather than supernatural explanations for the outcomes that they hear about or are shown.

Later findings have consolidated this basic conclusion. For example, Hickling and Wellman (2001) combed through children's everyday utterances, identified those in which children proposed an explanation for an outcome, and determined what kind of explanation they proposed. They found that children's explanations were mostly naturalistic and also appropriately domain-specific. For example, children tended to offer psychological explanations for psychological phenomena and biological explanations for biological phenomena. Admittedly, children often failed to supply a completely accurate explanation, but they were in the right ballpark and rarely resorted to invoking magic.

4.3 Impossible and Unusual Outcomes

To the extent that children discount the possibility of magical violations of everyday causality, and the evidence just reviewed indicates that they do, we can expect them to show a similar caution when asked about what can and cannot happen. More specifically, from an early age, children should differentiate between ordinary events that could happen because they do not fly in the face of any natural causal regularities and impossible events that could not happen precisely because they do go against such regularities. For example, they should agree that leaves could grow on a tree, whereas money cannot. Indeed, when Shtulman and Carey (2007) told children a story that included a mix of such ordinary and impossible outcomes, they were very accurate at differentiating between these two types of events. They said that the ordinary events could actually happen in real life but not the impossible events. This sharp differentiation was evident across a relatively wide age range – from five to eleven years. In fact, children were just as good at making the differentiation as adults. Moreover, this pattern is not confined to US children. Similar results emerged among children in Colombia. Like their US peers, they had no illusions about the possibility of money growing on trees (Orozco-Giraldo & Harris, 2019).

However, Shtulman and Carey observed a sharp age change when children were asked, not about impossible events, but about decidedly unlikely events, such as waking up and finding an alligator under your bed. Most younger children – five-year-olds – claimed that such an unlikely outcome could never happen. Rejection of the improbable was less marked as children got older, so that eleven-year-olds, just like adults, acknowledged that a variety of highly improbable events could actually happen.

This age change in thinking about the improbable is robust. Various follow-up studies have uncovered the same basic developmental pattern (Lane et al., 2016; Shtulman, 2009). How can we explain it? The findings discussed earlier suggest a plausible answer. When children imagine a possible scenario, as they do when they engage in pretend play, or envisage the future, they draw on their knowledge of reality. The possible or future events that they conjure up in their imagination do not depart very far from their past experience. When children are asked to say what can happen, their replies display a similar pattern of restraint. More specifically, their conservatism about unlikely happenings can be explained by supposing that children draw on their knowledge of past regularities. Asked whether leaves could grow on trees, they can draw on their knowledge of reality, readily envisage such a possibility in their imagination, having observed such a possibility many times, and come up with an affirmative answer. Asked whether money could grow on trees if they draw on their knowledge of reality, they will not be able to envisage such a possibility in their imagination and arrive at a negative answer. But similarly, when asked whether one might wake up and find an alligator under the bed if they draw on their knowledge of reality, they will again not be able to envisage such a possibility and arrive at a negative answer. In other words, children's conservatism about what can happen can be traced back to their limited imagination, which in turn owes its restrictions to their limited experience of reality. Indeed, children display a similar conservatism when asked to judge what entities exist. That conservatism can also be explained in terms of children's overreliance on their own knowledge and experience as a metric with which to evaluate the reality status of novel entities (Woolley & Ghossainy, 2013).

To briefly review: four- and five-year-olds have a considerable range of empirical experience. They draw on that empirical experience to make judgments about what can happen. This strategy serves them well in the sense that it leads them to exclude all sorts of impossible eventualities. We might say that children have their feet on the ground: They discount the possibility of magic, along with various outcomes that clearly violate the regularities they have observed in the past. At the same time, their feet are somewhat too firmly planted on the ground. They find it hard to imagine that anything unusual could actually happen. But, as they get older, this conservatism weakens and they admit that the improbable is not to be ruled out. It can happen.

4.4 Fairy Tales and Miracles

Given the power and ubiquity of fairy tales for young children, it is tempting to speculate that they portray a world to which young children are not just receptive but regard as an accurate portrayal of reality. This is indeed the conclusion that Bruno Bettelheim reached in his influential analysis of the appeal of fairy tales (Bettelheim, 1991). They portray, he argued, the world as children see it: prone to magical transformations and dramatic reversals of fortune, threatening and unpredictable. However, the findings discussed earlier cast doubt on Bettelheim's claims. Recall that various findings, including some that were available to Bettelheim, have shown that children rarely invoke magic, emphasizing instead naturalistic lines of explanation.

Granted the tension between Bettelheim's claim and children's skepticism about magic, it is worth posing the following question. If children are presented with a short story that contains fantastical or magical elements, how do they react? Do they assume that the characters and events in the story are realistic, as Bettelheim effectively implies? Alternatively, do they infer from the presence of fantastical or magical elements that the story must be a piece of fiction? Corriveau et al. (2009) presented young children with a mix of realistic and fantastical stories, embedding an unfamiliar character in each story. Children were asked to decide whether this unfamiliar character was a real person or a made-up person. Children aged five to six years were very systematic in sorting the characters and in justifying their sorting. They appropriately claimed that the characters in the realistic stories were real people and backed that up by pointing to telltale, realistic elements in the story (e.g., "He fought in the war."). By contrast, they said that the characters in the fantastical stories were made-up or "pretend" people and justified their answers by pointing to magical elements in the story (e.g., "There's no such thing as a special sword that could make you live forever."). These findings clearly cast doubt on Bettelheim's thesis: by the age of five or six, children treated the fairy-tale elements included in some of the stories as a clear indication that the story was not consistent with everyday reality. A follow-up study with Iranian children consolidated and extended this conclusion (Davoodi et al., 2016). Again, five- to six-year-olds differentiated between realistic and fantastical stories, associating real people with the former and pretend characters with the latter.

In summary, children around the age of five or six can conceptualize the fundamental difference between a narrative that recounts actual events and a narrative that recounts made-up or fictional events. That differentiation is intimately linked to their understanding of the difference between the kinds of ordinary events that take place in the real world and the kinds of extraordinary or magical events that can only take place in an unreal, fictional world.

However, as noted earlier, children are also presented with religious stories that recount miraculous events. How do young children respond to those stories? If children notice that such stories include events that do not, and indeed cannot, ordinarily happen, they will presumably regard them and the characters that they describe as equivalent to fairy tales. If, however, children are growing up in a religious family or community, and if they are receptive to the stance that is taken toward those stories by members of their family or community, they might regard such stories as factual or historical reports and not as fairy tales.

Studies of US children have provided a relatively clear resolution to this question (Corriveau et al., 2015). If children have not received any salient form or religious instruction – for example, if they do not go to church with their parents and are attending a state-run, secular school – they typically judge the main character in a miracle story to be a fictional or made-up character, and they justify that decision by reference to fantastical elements in the story, echoing the pattern seen in the earlier studies. If, however, they have received some form of religious instruction, either in school or by attending church (or both), they are more likely to regard the main character as a real person, someone capable of miraculous feats thanks to divine intervention. Indeed, a similar pattern is found irrespective of whether children are asked about the main character in the story or its central, miraculous event. Religious children (i.e., those who have received some form of religious education) are likely to judge both the character and the event as real, whereas children who have received no religious education are likely to see both as made up (Payir et al., 2021; Vaden & Woolley, 2011). At the same time, the impact of religious teaching appears to be circumscribed rather than pervasive. For example, when children were questioned about the likelihood of a desired outcome being brought about, children from highly religious backgrounds were more likely to predict that such outcomes would obtain following prayers – but they had no greater optimism in the efficacy of wish-making than their more secular peers (Lane, 2020). By implication, although religious instruction encourages children to believe in the power of divine intervention – it does not undermine children's broader understanding of causality and of the causal constraints on what can ordinarily happen.

Stepping back from these various findings, we can conclude that although there is no quick and simple answer to the question of what children think can happen, there is persuasive evidence that their horizon of possibilities expands. On the one hand, there is a robust developmental change: They become less skeptical about the remotely probable and increasingly acknowledge that it can sometimes happen. A plausible explanation for this developmental change is that children become increasingly reflective about the extent to which causal constraints might prevent a given outcome. When no such constraints are identified, they are prepared to acknowledge that something unlikely or untoward might come to pass even if they cannot specify exactly how (Harris, 2021).

There is also a culturally induced change. Absent a religious education, young children continue to doubt that miraculous violations of causal constraints can happen. However, in the wake of a religious education, such skepticism is often set aside. Children come to believe that the impossible can happen. However, this shift in children's conception of what is possible should not be overstated. A religious education leads children to be receptive to the possibility of divine intervention but, in other respects, it tends to leave their causal thinking intact. This divergence in the way that children think about miraculous possibilities is already present in the early school years and remains evident among older children (Payir et al., 2021).

4.5 Thought Experiments

A long tradition of educational thinking, reaching back to Piaget and Montessori, portrays young children as "hands-on" learners. The basic idea behind this characterization is that children learn best when they are actively engaged with the world, trying out various interventions, and observing what happens. Anyone who accompanies young children to a science museum will likely observe this educational philosophy on display. Museum educators go to considerable lengths to create exhibits that young children can interact with. Exhibits that children must not touch – but simply look at – are frowned upon.

However, the history of science shows that new insights are sometimes gained, not through hands-on, empirical investigation, but by engaging in thought experiments, by asking what would happen if a particular set of conditions were in place. In his dialogues, Galileo famously argued his case by appealing to thought experiments, for example, by asking about the speed with which two objects, one large and one small, would fall if they either fell separately or were yoked together.

Given the popular image of children as hands-on learners, there has been little research on the possibility that they, like adults, might also be able to arrive at new conclusions about the way the world works simply by engaging in a thought experiment. On the other hand, the preceding sections have emphasized that, when children are asked about what can and cannot happen, they are guided by their imagination, and that, in turn, their imagination is constrained by their observations of reality. Granted these points, it is reasonable to suppose that children's imagination can be used as a kind of virtual laboratory in which realistic scenarios can be played out, with the prospect that such scenarios might alert them to possibilities – or impossibilities – that they had not considered earlier. In short, it is feasible that children can benefit intellectually not just from hands-on investigation but also from engaging in thought experiments (Bascandziev & Harris, 2020; Lillard, 2001).

An initial indication that such learning was possible emerged in the context of research on the so-called tubes task. In that task, preschoolers are presented with an apparatus composed of three diagonally oriented, opaque tubes that crisscross each other. When a ball is dropped into the upper end of one tube, two- and three-year-olds often have trouble in figuring out where the ball will reemerge, frequently pointing to a tube-end positioned directly below the point of insertion even if that tube-end actually belongs to a different tube from the one into which the ball was dropped. The pattern of findings indicates that, based on their observation that most objects fall along a straight-down, vertical trajectory, children recruit that knowledge when anticipating where the ball will reemerge. Instead of recognizing that the ball will be constrained by the tube in which it is dropped to follow a diagonal rather than a vertical path, they plump for the more intuitive conclusion that it will end up at a point directly below the point of insertion, as if gravity were the only force to take into consideration (Hood, 1995, 1998; Hood et al., 2000).

In this context, empirical feedback has proven ineffective. When children are given several opportunities to look for the ball and discover where it actually ends up – that is, at the bottom end of whichever diagonal tube it was inserted into – they still persist in making incorrect, gravity-based predictions on later trials. By contrast, a less hands-on intervention has proven to be more helpful (Bascandziev & Harris, 2010). Three-year-olds were first given baseline trials in which, as expected, gravity-based errors were more frequent than correct answers. Next, children were given a brief verbal intervention. Some were offered only generic and unhelpful advice, "You have to pay attention to the tubes in order to find the ball." but others were offered more targeted advice. They were reminded that the ball would roll down the tube that it was dropped into or told to follow that tube with their eyes. This targeted advice proved effective. Whereas the children given generic advice showed no improvement in a posttest, the children given targeted advice produced more correct answers than gravity-based errors, reversing the pattern seen at baseline. A later study with two- and three-year-olds yielded similar results: When given pertinent, targeted advice about the trajectory of the ball ("The ball could not escape from this tube. It rolled inside this tube into this cup."), gravity errors were reduced (Bascandziev et al., 2016).

A plausible interpretation of this reduction is that the targeted advice prompted children to visualize the trajectory of the ball. More specifically, drawing on their longstanding grasp of the fact that one solid object cannot pass through another, children imagined the ball rolling diagonally down the length of the tube, rather than magically breaching the walls of the tube and falling in a straight-down, vertical trajectory. Consistent with this interpretation, Joh, Jaswal, and Keen (2011) found that, when they simply asked children before each test trial "Can you imagine the ball rolling down the tube?", gravity errors were again reduced. Indeed, there were revealing behavioral signs that children were benefiting from the experimenter's prompt to use their imagination. They often made an incorrect choice but then corrected themselves, whereas control children rarely displayed such second thoughts.

Taken together, these findings underline the possibility that children can advance conceptually simply by using their imagination (Bascandziev, 2021). As a strong test of this proposal, Bascandziev and Carey (2021) asked whether a thought experiment could help young children to overcome their naïve assumption that tiny amounts of matter – for example, a single grain of rice – weigh nothing at all. Children were presented with a kind of seesaw or teeter-totter, notably a central fulcrum (made of popsicle sticks glued together) with a long rectangular card placed crosswise so as to balance on the fulcrum. Children either watched what happened when successive grains of rice were placed on one side of the card so that it eventually tipped down as a result of their cumulative weight; alternatively, children were invited to simply imagine successive grains of rice placed on one side of the card but given no visible feedback as to the result. In either case, children frequently rejected their starting assumption that small amounts of matter weigh nothing. Thus, having either seen – or imagined – the difference that the addition of a single grain of rice could make to the equilibrium of the card straddling the central fulcrum, they changed their ideas about weight. They realized that if one grain of rice was enough to tip the card off balance, then one grain of rice must weigh something rather than nothing.

These findings showing that young children can learn from thought experiments vividly reinforce a central claim of this Element, namely that children's imagination, far from being wayward or fanciful, can and does mimic the forces and constraints that operate in the real world. As a result, it can serve as a mental laboratory or workshop, in which children have the possibility of discovering hitherto unrealized truths. The examples discussed here have involved children's grasp of physics – their understanding of a tube-constrained trajectory or the "weighty" impact of a grain of rice – but it is plausible that parallel results could be obtained in other domains, such as biology, psychology, and even morality.

4.6 Thinking about What Can Happen: Conclusions

When they try to envisage what will happen in the future, children, like adults, draw on their knowledge of the past. This basic claim has several ramifications. First, it means that children readily differentiate between prosaic events that could happen in the future – just as they have happened in the past – and impossible events that could not happen in the future – just as they have never happened in the past. Second, it means that young children are conservative about what can happen. They reject unusual events with which they have no prior experience as impossible, although this error abates with age. Third, given that what children imagine will happen is largely anchored to what they have actually observed to happen, their imagination can be used as a simulation device to envisage future possibilities. Indeed, when prompted to use their imagination in this fashion, children can discover things about the world that run counter to their less reflective intuitions. In this sense, young children are capable of, and can benefit from, thought experiments. Finally, this portrait of young children as clear-eyed realists needs to be tempered in one major respect. In the wake of religious instruction, but not in its absence, children come to believe that miraculous outcomes are possible, thanks to divine intervention.

5 Thinking about What Could Have Happened Instead

So far, I have asked mainly about children's forward-looking thoughts – their ideas about what could or could not happen in the future. But the imagination can also be deployed in a backward-looking fashion – to think about what did not actually happen but might have. Among adults, such counterfactual thoughts can entrain a good idea of emotion. In thinking about how we might have behaved differently, we may regret what we did. In thinking about how things could have turned out much worse than they did, we may feel relief at what transpired. By implication, our reflections and emotions with respect to the past often include a comparative element: We react to the differences between the actual course of events and an alternative or counterfactual reality that we entertain in our imagination. Do children engage in such counterfactual thinking, and if they do, how far do they resemble adults? For example, do they also feel regret or relief in light of a comparison between the actual and the counterfactual?

In an early probe into young children's ability to engage in counterfactual thinking, Harris et al. (1996) acted out various simple scenarios for preschoolers. For example, preschoolers watched as a doll called "Carol" walked across the kitchen floor, leaving visibly "muddy" footprints behind and were asked what would have happened if Carol had taken her shoes off before entering the kitchen. Children replied appropriately. They claimed that had she done so, the floor would now be clean rather than dirty. In another study, children were questioned to assess whether they would engage in counterfactual thinking with less explicit prompting. They were again presented with minor mishaps but in this study, they were asked to think about why the mishap had occurred and how it might have been prevented. For example, one story involved Sally who wanted to do a drawing. Her mother offered her a choice between a pencil and a black pen. Sally opted for the pen and ended up with inky fingers. Asked why the mishap occurred, children often referred to what Sally had *not* done: "She didn't draw with the pencil.", "She should've used the pencil." Children's citation of an alternative course of action was appropriately selective. If Sally's mother had initially offered her a choice between a blue pen and a black pen, they did not suggest that she should have made the alternative choice, presumably realizing that a pen of either color would have delivered an inky outcome.

Subsequent research on children's counterfactual thinking has extended these early findings in various ways. I focus on three main issues. First, some researchers have asked whether preschoolers engage in genuine counterfactual thinking or something more generic. Second, researchers have probed the emotional sequelae of counterfactual thinking by asking whether young children are prone to regret – or relief – when they think about how things might have gone differently. Third, pursuing a theme raised in the previous section, when children think about what might have happened, how far do their thoughts stray from ordinary reality. Do they think about relatively prosaic alternatives to what actually happened, or do they think about next-to-impossible or miraculous interventions?

5.1 Early Counterfactual Thinking?

Strictly speaking, counterfactual thinking involves thoughts about what would have happened if some specific aspect of what actually happened were altered. At first glance, children's reasoning about Carol's muddy shoes, and their realization that the kitchen floor would still be clean, had she removed her shoes seems to exemplify counterfactual thinking. However, it could be argued that children answered the experimenter's question by drawing on their general knowledge about muddy shoes and dirty floors, not their more specific knowledge about what Carol could have done even if she did not. For example, perhaps children thought to themselves: "Well, as long as you take your shoes off, the floor stays clean." In other words, maybe children did not ask themselves about Carol in particular ("What would have happened if Carol had taken her shoes off instead of keeping them on?") but simply thought about the consequences of shoe removal in general ("What happens if you take your shoes off?").

Indeed, subsequent experimental work suggested that young children might be resorting to this more generic strategy rather than a more targeted, counterfactual strategy (Rafetseder et al., 2013). For example, when they were presented with a scenario involving two dolls, Susie and Max, walking across the kitchen floor, each with muddy shoes, children still claimed – inaccurately – that had Max removed his shoes the kitchen floor would now be clean. By implication, children were misconstruing the question, treating it as a question about shoe removal in general rather than Max's shoes in particular.

However, other findings confirm that, provided preschoolers have a firm grip on the causal specifics of a situation, they do display counterfactual reasoning that is appropriate to the particulars of the situation under consideration. Nyhout and Ganea (2019) introduced preschoolers to an easy-to-understand apparatus – a box that lit up when blocks of a particular shape were placed on it – and demonstrated which blocks were effective and which were not. Two blocks were then placed on the box and children were questioned about what would have happened if only one rather than two had been placed on the box. When two causally effective blocks were placed on the box – so that it lit up – the majority of three-, four-, and five-year-olds realized that the removal of one of the two blocks would have no impact – the box would stay lit up. Furthermore, when children were asked questions about what would happen if two blocks, one effective and one ineffective, were placed on the box, four- and five-year-olds realized that the outcome of removing one block would depend on which particular block was removed. Thus, they grasped that the box would stay lit up if the ineffective block were removed but not if the effective block were removed. In summary, these studies indicate that preschoolers can engage in counterfactual thinking, at least in a situation where the impact of the causal elements is well understood.

5.2 Counterfactual Thinking and Emotion

Although feelings of regret are unpleasant, it is possible that regret is a healthy emotion in the sense that it might prompt us to review choices we have made and to behave differently in the future. Do children feel regret, and does it impact their subsequent behavior? Young children are not very good at realizing that another person might regret the choice that they made (Payir & Guttentag, 2019). However, when they are confronted with clear evidence that they themselves would have secured a better outcome if they had made a different choice, most children report feeling regret from the age of six upward. For example, faced with a choice between two boxes containing rewards that differ in value, five- and six-year-olds typically report feeling badly if, having chosen one box, they then learn that the other had a more desirable reward (McCormack et al., 2020; Weisberg & Beck, 2012). Presumably, in line with the capacities established in the preceding section, children's negative feelings are triggered by the counterfactual thought that, if they had chosen the other box, they would have received a better reward.

Adults might feel only fleeting regret in situations of random choice, such as the box studies just described. However, they might experience more lingering regret if they realize that greater consideration or reflection would have led them to act differently and secure a more desirable outcome. So, for example, when adults regret making a hasty purchase or regret not having persevered in a project, such feelings might prompt them to act differently in the future – when faced with a similar choice. Do children display this type of self-reflective regret, especially when they realize that they have acted impulsively or without sufficient reflection? McCormack and her colleagues (2019) created a variant of the box task to explore this possibility. Children aged six and seven were presented with two boxes and told that one box would automatically unlock after thirty seconds whereas the other would automatically unlock after ten minutes. An hourglass attached to each box helped children gauge the passage of time. Not surprisingly, most children opted for the short-delay box, sacrificing the opportunity to wait and open the other box. Of these children, some – but not all – reported feeling badly on learning that they would have received a better prize had they waited to open the other box.

The following day, children were given a similar choice between a short-delay and a long-delay box. As might be expected, children were more likely to opt for the long-delay box this time around. More importantly, however, the children who reported regret on the first day were especially likely to switch their choice on the second day. By implication, children are not only able to engage in counterfactual thinking about how they might have behaved differently, but they are also prone to experience the regret that can be triggered by such comparative thinking, and then to make a different choice when facing a similar choice again.

5.3 What Counterfactual Alternatives Do Children Bring to Mind?

Recall that in the study of preschoolers' reactions to mishaps, such as ending up with inky fingers, children spontaneously mentioned an alternative course of action when invited to think about why the mishap had befallen Sally (Harris et al., 1996). However, that alternative course of action was already fairly salient in the narrative. More specifically, children were told that Sally had chosen to draw with a pen rather than a pencil. So, children's imagination did not have to travel very far in order to identify a different course of action that she might have taken: It had already been mentioned in the story.

What happens when children are given no such hints? Do they still come up with an alternative course of action that the protagonist might have taken? Are these alternatives realistic or fanciful? And how far do the alternatives that children generate reflect the type of upbringing they have received? To explore these questions, Payir et al. (2022) presented six- to eleven-year-olds with stories involving a protagonist and a negative outcome, for example, a farmer named George whose strawberry plants had yielded no berries. After hearing a given story, children were asked to say what the protagonist might be thinking. So, with respect to farmer George, children were questioned as follows: "George said to himself, 'I could have had many berries, if ...' Can you guess how he finished his sentence?"

Irrespective of age, children almost always generated naturalistic alternatives: They proposed a practical course of action that the protagonist might have taken that would be likely to have delivered a better result, for example: "If only he had watered them more ... ." Children rarely suggested nonnaturalistic alternatives, such as: "He could have prayed for the rain." Indeed, across the hundreds of suggestions that children made, only a tiny fraction (2 percent) invoked some nonnatural or supernatural causal mechanism. These findings echo and extend the early studies conducted by Mead (1932) and Huang (1930). Not only do children mostly generate naturalistic explanations for why something happened, they also stick to naturalistic alternatives when thinking about how a negative outcome might have been prevented. Once again, we see that children's imagination is largely constrained by their knowledge of everyday reality. Contrary to popular stereotypes, they are not prone to flights of fancy or magical thinking.

However, this straightforward conclusion needs one intriguing qualification. After they had proposed alterative courses of action that the story protagonist might be contemplating, children were invited to assess various alternatives proposed by the experimenter. Overall, children remained receptive toward naturalistic alternatives but expressed skepticism toward nonnaturalistic alternatives. Nevertheless, there was an effect of prior religious instruction. As compared to children attending a secular school, those attending a parochial school were more likely to endorse the possibility of a divine intervention to bring about a different outcome. So, although religious instruction had no detectable impact on the counterfactual possibilities that children themselves generated, it did impact children's receptivity to suggestions put to them by an adult.

5.4 Thinking about Counterfactual Possibilities: Conclusions

The findings on children's counterfactual thinking reinforce and extend the findings that were reviewed in Section 4 regarding children's thinking about what might happen in the future. First, children are able to imagine the outcome of realistic or "near" counterfactuals, such as drawing with a pencil rather than a pen or removing a causally effective block rather than a causally ineffective block. Second, in contemplating such near counterfactuals, especially those involving a beneficial course of action that they could have taken – but did not – children are prone to experience and report feelings of regret. Moreover, such feelings of regret can prompt them to act differently when they are subsequently faced with a similar decision. Finally, when invited to propose an alternative course of action that an agent might contemplate in the wake of a negative outcome, children generate realistic and naturalistic alternatives. They do not wishfully invoke magical or fantastical possibilities. In summary, we see once more that children's imagination does not wander far from known and familiar pathways. There is one notable exception to this broad conclusion. Children who have had some form of religious instruction are more likely than children who have been reared in a predominantly secular environment to endorse the possibility that God might have intervened to bring about – in a miraculous fashion – a more benign outcome. Even here, however, this departure from natural reality should not be overstated. Left to their own devices, religious children rarely generated such departures themselves. It was only when they were invited to think about such divine interventions that they were ready to sanction them. Here, we see the gap between the scenarios that children imagine by themselves and the scenarios that the adult world invites them to contemplate. We will see other examples of this revealing gap in later sections.

6 Children's Imagination Infuses Their Interpretation of Reality

In the preceding sections, I have emphasized how children's encounters with, and their memory for, past reality are often recruited when they think about what can happen in the future or could have happened in the past. The implication of the findings reviewed is that the stock of information that children deploy when imagining future and past possibilities is frequently grounded – somewhat unadventurously – in what they have actually observed. According to this analysis, the portrait of young children as being lost in a fantasy or make-believe world is a caricature, and even a distortion, of their reality-oriented and predominantly commonsensical stance.

However, this analysis ends up obscuring an intriguing counterpoint. In the context of everyday conversation, children can often learn about entities or possibilities that are special or unusual. They may lie outside ordinary everyday experience, and they may even violate known causal constraints. For example, in previous sections, I noted that children's belief in God's extraordinary powers – a belief that is presumably not based on ordinary, everyday experience – can impact their thinking about future or counterfactual possibilities. In addition, in many cultures, children hear stories about special beings with magical powers. In some cases, they may be prompted to make active preparations for a visit from a special being, such as Santa Claus or the Tooth Fairy. In addition, they may be exposed to intriguing conversations about an unexpected appearance or disappearance. Finally, they may be encouraged to engage in games of make-believe that leave them half-hoping or half-fearing that what they are pretending is actually true.

In all these instances, the way that children appraise events and what they end up claiming about those events is often infused with ideas that have been planted in their imagination as a result of other people's suggestions, assertions, or questions. As noted, these ideas can include beings with special powers, ordinarily invisible agents, as well as unusual or mysterious happenings. As a result of this process of infusion, children sometimes end up claiming that they have witnessed – with their eyes and ears – what they almost certainly did not witness. In short, children's imagination can be stimulated by what other people say to them and in turn their imagination can infuse their interpretation of subsequent events. In the following sections, I discuss selected examples of this infusion process. Taken together, these findings temper the claim that young children always have their feet on the firm ground of reality.

6.1 Magical Transformations

In his fascinating "magic box" study, Subbotsky (1985) told children aged four to six years a story about a girl called Masha who was given a magic box that could change drawings of objects into the objects themselves. To do this, it was necessary to put a drawing in the box and pronounce the magic words "alpha beta gamma." At first, Masha was skeptical, but when she tested the box, she became convinced of its magical powers. Some days after hearing this story about Masha, the experimenter showed children a box and explained that it was "the same magic box that was given to Masha" and that if a picture of an object was put inside the box – for example, a picture of a flower – and the appropriate magic words were spoken the box could change the picture into the real thing, an actual flower. Children were then left alone with the box as well as pictures of various objects, effectively giving them an opportunity to try out the box for themselves. Presumably, at this juncture, children would have had two compet-ing impulses: on the one hand, to doubt that any such magical transformation was possible and on the other hand to wonder if – on the basis of what the experimenter had said – such transformations might be possible. In any case, once the experimenter had left, a considerable proportion of the children selected a picture of an attractive object – for example, a picture of a brooch rather than an insect – put it in the box and intoned the magic words. On reopening the box and discovering that the hoped for transformation had failed to occur, children expressed surprise and sometimes asked the experimenter on his return for more guidance about how to make the magic box work. Effectively, then, we see that an idea planted via the story about Masha, together with the experimenter's testimony about the provenance of the magic box, led children to expect a magical transformation. On opening the box and finding that no transformation of the picture had occurred – consistent, we may assume, with the overwhelming majority of past encounters with untransformable pic-tures – children were not always acquiescent. They held onto the idea that the box had a magical power and turned to the experimenter for guidance about what to try next. Here, then we have a simple but compelling example of the way in which the child's imagination, but more specifically, an idea planted in the child's imagination by the experimental context, infuses the child's inter-pretation of an ordinary event.

In a later study, children aged four to six were again introduced to an allegedly magical entity, namely, a liquid with the power to make an object travel back in time to an earlier state (Subbotsky, 1994). Children were given proof of its efficacy with the help of an old and crumpled postage stamp that was mysteriously returned to its pristine state when drops of the liquid were applied to it. In the wake of this combined testimony and demonstration, children's assumption that people cannot become younger was put to the test. The experi-menter made the following suggestion: "If you drink a little bit, you will probably turn into a little boy [girl]. Now you can try the water, if you want, I just want to see if it works. But if you don't want to try – it's up to you." Children were very reluctant to accept this invitation. By implication, despite their knowledge that children get older but never get younger, they were reluctant to run the risk of being transformed into a junior version of themselves. Again, we see that a counterintuitive idea, once planted in the child's imagin-ation, can infuse their interpretation of an otherwise commonplace event, namely, the invitation to have a drink.

6.2 Princess Alice Is Here

How do children respond when they are told about the presence of an invisible being? To explore this question, Bering and Parker (2006) invited children aged three- to nine years to play a guessing game. Before the game began, children in an experimental group were told about Princess Alice. Their attention was called to a picture of Princess Alice hanging on the back of the door, and they were told that she was in the room – despite being invisible – and would help them to play the guessing game. The guessing game itself was simple: While their back was turned, the experimenter claimed to put a ball in one of two boxes. On turning around, children were asked to guess which box the ball was in and to indicate their guess by placing their hand on the chosen box.

On selected trials, once children had signaled their guess with their hand, an unexpected physical event was made to occur. Either the picture of Princess Alice fell to the floor or a table lamp briefly flashed on and off. Bering and Parker (2006) analyzed children's behavior and reports for indications that they construed these unexpected events as helpful interventions by the invisible Princess Alice. Although the youngest children – three- to four-year-olds – rarely interpreted the unexpected events as having any connection to her, the oldest children – seven- to nine-year-olds – were likely to promptly move their hand to the other box and subsequently explain that the unexpected events were deliberate communications from Princess Alice (e.g., "Because she was telling me it was the wrong one."). Unsurprisingly, this pattern emerged only among children who had been forewarned of a possible intervention by Princess Alice. Children who had not been so warned treated the events as unexpected but straightforward physical events. Once again, these findings confirm that when children have been briefly primed by adult testimony to believe in an unusual and magical possibility, they are prone to accept that testimony and to construe subsequent events in light of what they have been told. Moreover, judging by the age change observed, this tendency to make a connection between an unexpected event and prior testimony waxes, rather than wanes with age.

Similar results were obtained in a follow-up study with five- to nine-year-olds (Piazza et al., 2011). Children were given the opportunity to win a prize by hitting the center of a target with a Velcro ball. Success was frustratingly unlikely because children had to throw from a distance, with their back to the target, using their nonpreferred hand. Not surprisingly, especially when they were left unsupervised, children often broke the rules and cheated in order to win, sometimes going so far as to walk up to the target and affix a ball to its center. However, children who had been told about the invisible presence of Princess Alice – and stated their belief in her existence – were much slower to resort to such cheating than unsupervised children. Indeed, they were as slow as children in a condition where an adult supervisor remained present. By implication, in the wake of the experimenter's testimony about Princess Alice, children varied in how they construed the act of cheating. Those who had been led to believe in the existence of Princess Alice were prone to think that their cheating would be seen and were more likely to refrain from cheating as a result.

Taken together, the Princess Alice studies underline the power of the infusion process and the different forms it can take. In both studies, children were led to accept the presence of an invisible person even though invisibility is clearly not a routine characteristic of human beings. Furthermore, having accepted the idea of her presence, children went on to interpret events and potential actions in light of her assumed presence – on the one hand, they treated unexpected events as helpful communications from Princess Alice, and on the other hand, they worried that she would know if they ventured to cheat.

6.3 A Visit from the Tooth Fairy

One of the most detailed and convincing examples of the infusion process is reported by Principe and Smith (2008a). Rather than probing the impact of an idea deliberately planted in a laboratory setting by an experimenter, they took advantage of the fact that young children routinely learn about an important special being, notably the Tooth Fairy, typically from their parents. On the basis of an initial interview, five- and six-year-olds could be assigned to three levels of belief in the Tooth Fairy – believers, uncertains, and disbelievers. Children were then asked to describe what had happened on the most recent occasion when they had lost a primary tooth. Their reports were scored for the extent to which they mentioned: (i) realistic aspects of what had happened (e.g., wiggling a loose tooth until it came out); (ii) ritualistic aspects (e.g., putting a tooth under the pillow); and (iii) fantastical aspects (e.g., claiming that the Tooth Fairy had flapped her wings). Children in the three belief categories were equally likely to refer to ritualistic aspects but differed with respect to the other two aspects. The more children had expressed skepticism about the Tooth Fairy, the more they were likely to mention realistic aspects of her visit. By contrast, the more children believed in the Tooth Fairy the more they were likely to mention fantastical aspects of her visit. Their reports were not always pure and simple eyewitness recollections of what had actually happened at the last visit – they were colored by the beliefs that children held about such visits.

The impact of children's beliefs on their memory for the visit was especially evident in a more detailed analysis of children's references to any fantastical aspects. These references were scored for explicit allusions to either *seeing* the Tooth Fairy during her visit ("When she went out the window, I *saw* her little sparkle and she flied like this (demonstrates) with her wand.") or to *hearing* the Tooth Fairy ("I *heard* her creeping in my room."). Not surprisingly, both types of reference increased with level of belief. Moreover, children whose parents had surreptitiously provided more confirmatory evidence of the Tooth Fairy's visit (e.g., a sprinkling of fairy dust) were more likely to assert that they had seen her. In summary, children's belief that the Tooth Fairy is real, especially when bolstered by parent-supplied "evidence," led them to report observational evidence of her visit. Consistent with other studies of children's testimony (Principe & Schindewolf, 2012), these findings confirm that children's eyewitness (or earwitness) testimony needs to be taken with several grains of salt. The ideas that they acquire on the basis of parent-supplied testimony and planted "evidence" lead them to supplement their reports with imaginary elements.

However, in defense of the fanciful accounts produced by these five- and six-year-old believers, one might argue that their claims of having actually seen or heard the Tooth Fairy were largely based on the way that they had glossed the experimenter's invitation to describe her most recent visit. Perhaps children thought they should amplify their reports by adding in some vivid details about what had happened. In other words, perhaps these observational claims were included because of their notions about what counts as "a good story." After all, adult raconteurs do not always stick to reporting exactly what they have observed – as storytellers, they tend to have, or take, some license to embroider and exaggerate. On this more sympathetic interpretation, children's misleading claims to have seen or heard the Tooth Fairy were not ultimately due to any confusion in their own minds about what had actually happened, nor indeed to any deliberate intention to mislead but rather to a lively sense of the storyteller's art.

To assess this possibility, Principe and Smith (2008b) conducted a follow-up study in which they took pains to signal the kind of report that they wanted children to provide. More specifically, some children were asked to provide a true report, with the interviewer reminding them: "I like children who tell exactly true stories." Other children, by contrast, were asked to provide a fun report, with the interviewer reminding them: "I like children who tell really fun stories." In addition, children were grouped – as in the earlier study – into believers, uncertains, and disbelievers. The key results emerged from the believers: No matter what type of story they were prompted to tell, a true story or a fun story, a good deal of what they said – much more than for the disbelievers – was fantastical (about 45 percent). Thus, the believers were prone to report fantastical aspects of the visit even when asked to stick to the sober truth. By implication, they were prone to think that these fantastical elements had actually occurred – they were not simply trying to tell a good story. A similar pattern emerged when children's reports of seeing or hearing the Tooth Fairy were examined. Irrespective of the type of story they were asked for, most believers claimed to both hear and see the Tooth Fairy, whereas very few of the disbelievers did so.

In fact, it was the uncertain children rather than the believers or disbelievers who were especially prone to tailor their story to the interviewer's preference, often including fantastical elements as well as claims about seeing and hearing the Tooth Fairy when asked to tell a fun story but not when asked to tell a true story. By implication, in their uncertainty, they took their cue about what to report from the interviewer, embroidering their narratives with fantastical elements when prompted to tell a fun story but stripping those away when prompted to tell a true story. The believers, by contrast, produced elaborations inadvertently, being unable to differentiate between what they had actually observed and what they were making up. The disbelievers restricted themselves to the sober truth, avoiding any fanciful elaboration.

Granted that believers were prone to make things up, including claims of having seen or heard the Tooth Fairy, when exactly in the sequence of events might they have done so? As Principe and Smith (2008b) noted, we cannot be sure. Maybe the ideas that children held about the Tooth Fairy prompted them to indulge their imagination on the night that they were expecting her visit, leading them to see and hear things that did not actually occur or perhaps to misinterpret suggestive sights and sounds. Alternatively, children's beliefs may have led them to engage in some reconstructive elaboration when they were providing their report. In thinking back to what had happened, they may have imagined sights and sounds that were plausible, given their beliefs in the actual existence of the Tooth Fairy, and then proceeded to report those imaginings as veridical. In either case, we can conclude that children's imagination, guided by their ideas about the Tooth Fairy and her powers, infused their memory for what actually happened and who was responsible – even if we cannot pinpoint when exactly that infusion process occurred.

Summarizing across the various studies described so far, it is clear that, when children are presented with misleading testimony by adults with regard to unusual or magical possibilities, their imagination subsequently goes to work, actively infusing their construal of otherwise naturalistic events. They readily imagine the presence or agency of the special being in question. Thus, they infer that – despite her invisibility – Princess Alice provided helpful signals via unusual and unexpected events or will be cognizant of their transgressive behavior. In the case of the Tooth Fairy, they go so far as to claim that they have seen or heard her. Still, it is important to underline two notable constraints on such imaginative infusion. First, there is little evidence of any autonomous invention by children in these studies. They do not spontaneously imagine the possibility of magical transformations or special beings. Instead, those ideas are conveyed to them, in the first instance, by adults. Moreover, that adult testimony is sometimes reinforced by suggestive physical evidence, planted or contrived by the adults in question. Second, children's imagination impacts their construal of otherwise naturalistic events only insofar as they accept and believe in the testimony that adults have provided. Thus, when children imagine particular events to have taken place – for example, that the Tooth Fairy flew in the bedroom window – those imaginings are grounded in their belief that the being in question actually exists. Similarly, when children resist the impulse to win a prize via cheating, that resistance is seen among believers in Princess Alice but not among skeptics. Stated differently, there is little indication that children are engaging in idle or playful fantasizing when they invoke such special beings or construe events and potential actions in light of their existence. They are invoking ideas that they take to be part of reality.

6.4 Magic Mumfry's Missing Rabbit

As noted, a striking feature of the results reported by Principe and Smith is that, once an idea is planted, it can impact not just children's interpretation of somewhat ambiguous events – such as a falling picture – it can also impact what children claim to have witnessed firsthand. Recall that children who believed in the Tooth Fairy were prone to claim that they had seen or heard her during her visit. However, it could be argued that such infusion effects, especially the effects on reported perceptual experience, are likely to be quite rare. Specifically, perhaps such effects occur only when children are presented with an intriguing idea via adult testimony. Recall that in all the studies just described, children had been given information either by an experimenter or by their parents. Presumably, children treated these adults as reliable and trust-worthy sources of information, so that the claims they made were treated as veridical. Accordingly, it is tempting to assume that infusion effects do occur when adults make misleading assertions but are likely to be rare in other circumstances.

However, infusion effects are not, in fact, confined to information transmitted by adults. Principe and her colleagues (2006) asked how far children can be swayed not just when ideas are planted by apparently trustworthy adults but also by their peers. In the first part of the study, preschoolers enjoyed a visit from Magic Mumfry, a magician who performed a variety of tricks. Sadly, his finale –

involving the production of a rabbit from his hat – was a failure. Despite several attempts, Magic Mumfry was unable to make the rabbit materialize. Subsequently, different groups of children received varying accounts as to the whereabouts of the missing rabbit. Some children got to eavesdrop on a conversation between two teachers in which it was alleged that the missing rabbit had been spotted in a nearby classroom. Other children did not hear this adult conversation, but as classmates of those who did, they were likely to learn about the location of the missing rabbit from them. Finally, there were two control groups: in one, children were not supplied with any information about the rabbit, whereas in the other, children got to actually see, rather than hear about, the rabbit's presence in a classroom.

Some weeks later, when children were interviewed about what had happened, the groups varied sharply in their reports. Thus, in response to a neutral interview, in which no suggestive questions implying the rabbit's presence in the classroom were posed, children who had not been given any information about the rabbit's appearance in the classroom never claimed to have seen it, whereas children who had seen it always reported doing so. This bifurcation is, of course, exactly what one would predict if children were trustworthy eyewitnesses. However, the results for the eavesdroppers and their classmates were unexpected: Among the eavesdroppers, nearly 40 percent said they had seen the rabbit in the classroom, and among their classmates, more than 66 percent did so. In short, when children heard a conversation indicating the location of the missing rabbit, they not only absorbed this idea, it infused their reports about what they had observed for themselves. Moreover, contrary to the speculation that such infusion effects would only occur in the wake of apparently reliable adult testimony, the classmates who learned about the rabbit's location only from their peers were just as susceptible to such effects as the eavesdroppers on an adult conversation. By implication, especially perhaps when there is a mystery, children readily take up another person's suggestion, including a suggestion made by another child; echoing the findings for the Tooth Fairy, children claim to have witnessed what they manifestly did not.

6.5 Just Pretending?

Surveying the various results reported so far, it could be objected that the child's imagination is not really a necessary or active component in the infusion process. Instead, it could be argued that children are simply responsive to others' affirmative testimony. Whether that testimony is provided by an experimenter, a parent, or another child, children often end up believing it. Indeed, everyday observation and experimental studies (Woolley, Boerger & Markman, 2004) confirm that children readily come to believe in special beings in the wake of others' testimony. Arguably, it is the beliefs that children form on the basis of such testimony, rather than any act of the imagination, that shapes how they interpret and report on subsequent events. Given this objection, it is worth asking how children respond not to affirmative testimony but instead to a simple invitation to engage in an act of imagining.

In one such experiment, four- and six-year-olds were given such an invitation (Harris et al., 1991). They were first shown two large boxes and encouraged to check that both were empty. Next, the experimenter invited children to pretend that there was a creature inside one of the boxes – either a friendly rabbit or a mean monster – and then explained that she was going to fetch a gift. Before leaving, she asked the children if there was really a rabbit or a monster in the box or if they were just pretending, and as expected, almost all the children said that they were just pretending. A camera captured children's behavior during the two-minute absence of the experimenter. Almost half opened either one or both boxes, with a shorter latency to open the box housing the pretend creature. When the experimenter came back and questioned them, approximately half of the children said that they were sure that there was nothing inside the box, but the remaining children admitted to having wondered if there was a creature inside, despite their earlier insistence that they were only pretending.

In a subsequent study with three- to seven-year-olds, these individual differences were examined in more detail (Johnson & Harris, 1994). Children were again presented with two boxes, asked to pretend that there was either a fairy or some ice cream in one of them, and filmed during the experimenter's brief absence. On her return, the experimenter probed children in some detail about their thoughts and actions during her absence. On the basis of their replies, they could be assigned to two main groups. More than half the children were open-minded and curious – they admitted to wondering if there was something inside the box, often justifying their stance by reference to magical or special processes (e.g., "She . . . flew in the box when I opened it but I didn't see her 'cos she's tiny."). Slightly fewer than half were skeptical – they were confident that there was nothing in the box, typically citing straightforward physical considerations (e.g., "It was empty before."). Finally, a small residue of children wavered in their replies. As might be expected, the open-minded and skeptical children behaved differently while the experimenter was absent. Most of the open-minded children investigated the pretend box – only a few ignored it. By contrast, the majority of the skeptical children ignored the pretend box – only a minority opened it.

In summary, although the infusion process is often set in motion by affirmative testimony by other people with respect to the existence of special beings or magical processes, it can also be triggered – at least among some children – if they are invited to engage in a simple act of imagining.

6.6 Imagination and Infusion: Conclusions

In earlier sections, I emphasized that, when children engage in an act of the imagination – for example, when they engage in pretend play, envisage the future, or contemplate counterfactual possibilities – children draw much of their inspiration from their observation and knowledge of reality. In that sense, children can be characterized as realists rather than fantasists. Nevertheless, the studies recounted in this section have revealed an important exception to children's ordinarily commonsensical stance. In response to misleading assertions by other people or indeed in response to an invitation to simply imagine something that is not true, the ideas that are thereby implanted can infuse children's later behavior and reports. They try out an allegedly magical box; they cautiously refuse a supposedly rejuvenating potion; they claim to have observed the Tooth Fairy or a conjuror's missing rabbit when they have not; and they entertain the possibility that a creature or a fairy has somehow found its way into a box they reported as empty approximately one minute earlier.

A final clarification is worth noting. The experiments described in this section have focused on children, but there is no reason to suppose that the infusion process that has been highlighted disappears in the course of development. Indeed, Subbotsky (2001) reports that adults can be primed to entertain the possibility of magical processes, especially as indexed by their nonverbal reactions

7 Absorption in an Imaginary World

The discussion so far, especially the discussion of children's thoughts about what might happen in the future or what might have happened in the past, has not paid much attention to the incidence and phenomenology of sustained immersion in a make-believe world. Yet from an intuitive standpoint, it is that feature of the imagination which makes it especially intriguing. Whether we watch a young child lost in a book or reflect on our own immersion in a film or a television series, the fact that imaginary worlds can be so engaging is worth dwelling on (Harris, 1998). Indeed, one might reasonably object that the analyses presented so far cast no light on that state of absorption – as I propose to call it – precisely because the mental processes that have been discussed so far are closely tethered to ongoing reality. Thoughts about the future, or about what might have happened in the past, rarely venture very far from what is known about reality.

By contrast, when children or adults are absorbed by a make-believe world, thoughts about current or recent reality may be surrendered for some length of time. Indeed, it is precisely the happy suspension of ongoing concerns that makes the make-believe world so appealing.

Once we do focus on that state of absorption, a series of questions arises. First, although it is intuitively obvious that adults and children are readily absorbed by an imaginary or fictional world, is there some telltale signature of that state beyond our subjective self-reports of feeling absorbed? Does the state come with a distinctive phenomenology, and is the profile of that state roughly the same whether we are talking about toddlers engaged in make-believe play, a child reading *Harry Potter*, a teenager playing a video game, or an adult watching *Downton Abbey*? Second, are there individual differences in the susceptibility to absorption, and if so, how exactly do individuals vary? Do they vary in the intensity of their absorption, in their frequency, or in the type of material that they are absorbed by? Third, can we arrive at some tentative characterization of what is happening when we are absorbed in an imaginary world? Do we simply mean that the imaginary world is vivid and salient to us, or is something else going on?

7.1 Signs of Absorption

Much of the time, the emotions and concerns that we experience are provoked by the opportunities and challenges that we – or those in our circle – face in the real world. We worry about an upcoming interview, rejoice at an unexpected success, lament a perceived injustice, feel relief at meeting a deadline, and so forth. However, our mental transportation into an imaginary world can temporarily override our default tendency to be preoccupied by real-world concerns (Green, Brock & Kaufman, 2004). Once we are so absorbed, it is the opportunities and challenges facing the protagonists in that imaginary world that drive our emotional reactions. We temporarily suspend our own concerns and become engaged with those that arise in the fictional world. This aspect of absorption seems to be a developmental constant. Whether we focus on toddlers, children, or adults, there appears to be a great deal of continuity in the tendency to be engaged by the fate of individuals who exist only in the imagination. Admittedly, older children and adults are probably more adroit in calibrating their exact degree of engagement – more likely than younger children to remind themselves that the plight they are so moved by concerns a fictional protagonist in a story or movie rather than a real person (Harris, 2000). However, this developmental change in the ability to regulate our emotional reactions to fiction does not threaten the claim that throughout development, fictions frequently engage their audience and provoke emotion.

This psychological continuity with respect to engagement and emotion undermines a common trope about early childhood. Noting their strong emotional reactions to a sad or frightening episode in a storybook, it can be tempting to conclude that children's emotional engagement is the result of a confusion about the difference between the real world and a make-believe world. But we often see similarly potent reactions among adults. Indeed, various adult-oriented genres – thrillers, horror stories, tragedies, and feel-good comedies – are categorized in terms of the particular emotional reactions that they elicit from readers or viewers. Among adults, we see such emotional reactions occurring even though it is unlikely that they are confused about the difference between the real world and a make-believe world. They know that the heroine is battling imaginary rather than actual aliens. By implication, being emotionally engaged by make-believe events is a pervasive disposition among humans of all ages – not because they are confused about the status of those make-believe events but despite being lucid about their status.

7.2 Absorption: State or Trait?

In a fascinating, retrospective study, Hilgard (1970) interviewed hundreds of Stanford undergraduates about their childhood and found that their tendency to become absorbed in a hypnotically suggested experience as young adults was associated with a history of imaginative involvements as a child. By implication, there are individual differences in the tendency to become absorbed in an ongoing experience, including the experience of a make-believe world, and it is possible that those individual differences remain stable across childhood and into adulthood. Partly in the wake of Hilgard's pioneering research, personality scales have been developed expressly aimed at the measurement of such involvement. The Tellegen absorption scale has proven to be an especially influential instrument (Tellegen & Atkinson, 1974).

Informal observation of young children suggests that, in line with Hilgard's findings, there are individual differences in imaginative engagement, especially when it comes to reading. Some children are avid readers: They like nothing better than curling up with a book, immersing themselves in its fictive world, and ignoring real-world distractions. Other children rarely read a book from one year to the next. It is tempting to think that avid readers are avid readers precisely because they are more susceptible to the type of imaginative absorption that was first described by Hilgard whereas nonreaders are not. It is worth asking however if we should think of absorption as a state that many children can enter into given an appropriately engaging context – or video game or book – not as a trait possessed by a small minority of children. Consider the phenomenon of Harry Potter. By the age of eight, 15 percent of US children have read one of the Harry Potter books. By the age of seventeen, almost half (49 percent) have done so, according to an online survey reported by Watson (www.statista.com/statistics/689693/kids-read-harry-potter-books-by-age-group/).

Reading a Harry Potter book would appear to call for protracted absorption: They are not short. The last four volumes of the series are each well over 700 pages long. Indeed, such has been their impact on children's reading – and on astute publishers – that children's books have grown in length in the United States. In 1986, a children's book was on average 137 pages long; a decade later in 1996, little had changed – it was on average still only 137 pages long. In 2006, however, the average length was 174 pages, and in 2016 it was 290 pages. Book length more than doubled in the twenty-year period between 1996 and 2016. A plausible explanation is that Harry Potter was starting to weave his magic, especially when we note that the first Harry Potter novel was published in the United States in 1998 – shortly after the start of this twenty-year period – under the title *Harry Potter and the Sorcerer's Stone*. At 320 pages, this was the shortest book in the series, but it was still more than twice as long as the average children's book published in the preceding two decades.

When we consider the number of children who have read a Harry Potter book, and the fact that books in the series range from 320 to 768 pages, we are pushed to the conclusion that, notwithstanding Hilgard's early focus on individual differences, getting lost in a book is not an especially unusual phenomenon. Even if we make the skeptical assumption that half the children who claim to have read a Harry Potter book never actually finished it, we are still left with a figure of just under 25 percent of the US child population who did finish it – and that figure will surely include many children who finished not one but several books in the series. Admittedly, we do not know if Harry Potter aficionados are prone to exactly the same state of absorption as more regular and avid readers of fiction, but it seems reasonable to assume that there is at least some overlap. In short, there are good grounds for arguing that the tendency to become engaged in an imaginary world is not confined to a small, absorption-prone minority of children but rather is a state that can be attained by a large proportion of the child population – at least, when they are in the hands of a master storyteller like J. K. Rowling.

A study exploring absorption in a story world among nine- and ten-year-old children supports this argument (Prezioso, 2022). After indicating whether they were avid or non-avid readers (as indexed by the frequency with which they read for pleasure each week), participants responded to a questionnaire adapted from Kuijpers et al. (2014). Specifically, they were asked to report on four dimensions of their experience of absorption – notably, attention, transportation, emotional engagement, and mental imagery – when reading their favorite, most immersive book. Both avid and non-avid readers reported similarly high levels of absorption, particularly in the domains of attention, emotional engagement, and mental imagery. For example, 71 percent of the avid readers and 70 percent of the non-avid readers answered either "agree" or "strongly agree" to the statement: "After I finished the story, I kept thinking about what happened in the story." Similarly, 77 percent of the avid readers and 75 percent of non-avid readers answered either "agree" or "strongly agree" to the statement: "I felt connected to the main character or some of the other characters." Beyond these questionnaire items, when participants were interviewed about their reading experience, avid and non-avid readers described the feeling of absorption similarly. For example, one avid reader mentioned that she "didn't realize how long she had been reading" and "wanted to know what happened next." Similarly, a non-avid reader explained that she "couldn't let go" of the story because she needed to discover subsequent plot details. Based on these findings, it is plausible that children can experience absorption in a story world no matter whether they are avid or occasional readers. More specifically, some books are so engrossing that they "hook" even the most occasional readers.

7.3 Psychological Characteristics of Absorption

Granted that absorption is not some exotic state confined to a small minority of children, what are its psychological characteristics? Classic work on text comprehension provides some suggestive clues. In a series of studies, Bower and his colleagues showed that, when adults read a text describing a protagonist moving through a terrain, their center of consciousness travels along with the protagonist (Bower & Morrow, 1990). If readers are asked about the presence or absence of particular landmarks in the terrain, the length of time that they take to give an answer depends on the distance of those landmarks from the protagonist. Questions about landmarks that are close to the protagonist are answered quickly, whereas questions about landmarks that are more distant are answered more slowly. A simple but compelling example of this phenomenon of moving consciousness was reported by Glenberg et al. (1987). Participants were presented with a text about a jogger either removing or putting on a sweatshirt before setting off around the running track. When participants read the text and were probed about the sweatshirt, they were faster to reply when the jogger was wearing the sweatshirt as compared to when he had left it behind.

By implication, readers "accompany" a protagonist through his or her world; items close to the protagonist are foregrounded in consciousness such that readers can more rapidly answer questions about them.

Further evidence for this process of "accompaniment" comes from studies on readers' responses to so-called deictic verbs of motion (i.e., those verbs that presuppose a direction of travel toward, e.g., *come*, *bring*, or away, e.g., *go*, *take*, from a given point of origin). When adult readers were told about a movement toward or away from the main protagonist in a text, they understood and remembered that movement better if the deictic verb was appropriately tailored to the locus of the protagonist (Black et al., 1979). A similar pattern has emerged when children listen to a story (Rall & Harris, 2000). Consider the following mini episode: "Little Red Riding Hood was sitting in her bedroom when her mother came in and asked her to go Grandmother's house." When children listened to this story fragment and were asked to retell it in their own words, they typically did so quite accurately. But consider this subtly different phrasing: "Little Red Riding Hood was sitting in her bedroom when her mother *went* in and asked her to go to Grandmother's house." When asked to retell this version, children were prone to make a revealing error in their recall: they often switched the deictic verbs, replacing *went* with *came*.

Why exactly did children make such substitution errors? The most plausible explanation is that when they start listening to a story, in line with the proposals made by Bower and his colleagues, children's center of consciousness is not static but mobile. Effectively, children travel in their imagination to the setting in which the protagonist is located. So, listening to the episode about Little Red Riding Hood, they imagine themselves in her bedroom rather than in some distant or neutral location. Then, from that vantage point, they process subsequent events and movements accordingly. For example, when they hear about Little Red Riding Hood being asked by her mother to go to her grandmother's house, they encode that request as the consequence of her mother's approach rather than her departure (i.e., as a "coming" – not as a "going" – into her bedroom).

However, there is a powerful objection to this analysis, especially as an account of how young children process fiction: It seems to fly in the face of classical accounts of early childhood cognition. According to a long tradition of experimental work with preschoolers, they are prone to egocentrism, a tendency to stay rooted in their own spatial and visual perspective, combined with a difficulty in imagining how the world might appear to someone elsewhere with a different vantage point. However, there is a plausible counter to this objection. In studies of childhood egocentrism, children are seated on one side of a given array, and they are then asked to imagine what it looks like to someone seated on the other side of that same visible array. When children become imaginatively engaged in a story, however, something different is going on. They are not being invited to mentally contemplate how current reality would look from a different vantage point. They are being invited to set current reality aside in its entirety – the chair they are sitting on, the adult nearby who is reading to them – and to position themselves in an imaginary world, for example, a world that includes Little Red Riding Hood's cottage and indeed Little Red Riding Hood herself sitting in her bedroom. In short, children appear to find it easy to set current reality temporarily aside and to adopt the protagonist's perspective in an imaginary world. They are capable of that imaginary displacement even if, when contemplating reality itself, they find it difficult to abandon their particular perspective, for example, the perspective from one side of an actual table, so as to adopt a different perspective on the other side of that same actual table.

Follow-up studies have confirmed and extended these findings on children's story comprehension. Ziegler et al. (2005) raised the possibility that children only show such perspective-taking when they are familiar with the story in question. Indeed, children's tendency to adopt the perspective of the main protagonist might occur only when they know the story well enough to retrieve the sequence of events from long-term memory. On this view, perspective-taking errors in recall would not occur if children were presented with novel stories that they had never heard before. However, in line with the findings with adults, young children (ranging from four to nine years) continued to make substitution errors when they listened to unfamiliar stories that included an inconsistent deictic verb. For example, presented with the following sentence – "Laura was sitting in the lounge looking at a picture book when Tony went into the room." – they tended to substitute *came* for *went* in their recall. They scarcely ever made such errors when the deictic verb was consistent. By implication, the tendency to imaginatively share the perspective of the protagonist does not depend on priming by a familiar story but is a more or less immediate strategy as soon as a text is encountered and a main protagonist is identified.

Nonetheless, one might suspect that children's perspective-taking will be immediate and effective if the character they first hear about appears to be a good person rather than a bad person. After all, most fiction, especially fiction for children, tends to present long-suffering, brave, or likable characters as the main protagonists in a story rather than wicked stepmothers. It is possible, however, that perspective-taking is mainly driven by more automatic, nonevaluative processes. In particular, it is feasible that the way that a story is set up has a potent effect. For example, the first character to be introduced might determine subsequent processing. To compare these two possibilities, Ziegler et al. (2005) varied not only the deictic verb but also the standing of the main character – with one being a good character, notably a prince, and the other being a more dubious character, notably a ghost. The results were clear-cut. No matter whether the first character to be introduced was a prince or a ghost, children processed the text from that character's perspective. On the other hand, when the story started by introducing a nonhuman character, namely a toy car, perspective-shifting was reduced, as one might expect.

Finally, consistent with the proposal that young children spontaneously adopt the spatial perspective of the main protagonist, Ziegler and Acquah (2013) showed that the speed and accuracy with which children answer questions about the location of objects within an imagined scene reflect biases inherent in the protagonist's perspective on that scene. Thus, consistent with the dominance of the front-back axis over the left-right axis (Bryant, Tversky & Franklin, 1992), children were quicker and more accurate in answering questions about objects positioned in front of or behind the protagonist as opposed to objects positioned to the left or right of the protagonist. Moreover, this front-back bias emerged even though children were told that the protagonist made successive turns, thereby altering which particular objects were located along the front-back axis as compared to the left-right axis. These findings provide persuasive evidence that young children view an imagined scene from the inside – seeing it as the protagonist sees it.

The findings so far have highlighted cognitive processes – mental displacements within the fictional world of the story protagonist. Is there any evidence for more visceral reactions when children enter an imaginary world? Solid, experimental evidence is surprisingly sparse, but there are some suggestive findings. Thibodeau-Nielsen et al. (2020) presented three- to five-year-olds with fantasy story prompts (e.g., "One day, you and your friends rode a spaceship to the moon ... ") accompanied by a suitable picture and encouraged them to elaborate on the story prompt (e.g., " ... tell me more about what happens."). Sympathetic nervous system activity, as indexed by tonic changes in skin conductance levels, increased during children's narrations, as compared to a control task in which children were simply asked to verbally identify objects depicted in a picture. Moreover, this difference was found across children, no matter how engaged they appeared in responding to the story prompt, and also irrespective of the emotional valence of their elaboration and its judged creativity. Thus, when children generated and described an imaginary scene, they displayed more arousal than when they observed and described a visible scene. In future research, it will be interesting to find out if arousal varies depending on whether children listen to a narrative prompting engagement with a protagonist as compared to a control narrative lacking a protagonist.

7.4 Absorption in an Imaginary World: Conclusions

Young children, like adults, are prone to become absorbed in an imaginary world, especially a story world. When so absorbed, their center of consciousness appears to temporarily leave real-world concerns behind and to "live" temporarily alongside the fictional protagonists. Although informal observation indicates that there are marked individual differences among children in the frequency with which they become absorbed in a fictional world, that state appears to be within reach of most children, as revealed by the wide-ranging appeal of certain stories and novels as well as the firsthand reports of avid and occasional readers alike. The process of absorption is not well understood, but the notion of mental transportation is not entirely metaphorical. In processing a text, listeners and readers appear to temporarily position themselves within the imaginary world such that the relative salience of landmarks and events within it is based on the standpoint of the main protagonist.

8 Creativity in Young Children

Young children like to play and, as discussed, pretend play is common in early childhood, irrespective of whether the adult world does or does not supply scaffolding and support. Early childhood educators sometimes express anxieties about the consequences of curtailing the opportunities for play, especially pretend play. Alongside such concerns, a more radical stance is sometimes adopted, both by child psychologists and educators, namely, that childhood is a time when we human beings are especially creative and inventive but subjection to an overly academic curriculum dulls children's natural creativity. In an engaging TED talk, the former education adviser to the UK government, Sir Ken Robinson, laid out these claims (www.ted.com/talks/sir_ken_robinson_ do_schools_kill_creativity?language=en). The talk has been watched by more than seventy million viewers, suggesting that his message has wide appeal. However, it relies on anecdote, mordant humor, and impeccable timing rather than psychological evidence. It is worth pausing, therefore, to take a closer look at the available findings on creativity and inventiveness in childhood. None of the findings deals a lethal blow to Robinson's stance, but they do show that his case is less convincing that it might first appear. Rather than waning, children's inventiveness increases with age. To illustrate that age change, I describe research on children's readiness to create a problem-solving tool and to produce a nonfigurative drawing.

8.1 Inventing Tools

In recent decades, thanks to the pioneering work of Jane Goodall and bolstered by pooled data from many primate field sites, we have come to accept that humans are not the only toolmakers on the planet. Our nonhuman cousins also make and use tools, to "fish" for food in termite mounds, for example, or to "sponge" up liquids. Indeed, toolmaking is not confined to primates – crows are smart enough to fashion a hook from wire so as to retrieve an otherwise inaccessible reward. At the same time, the greater complexity of human tools is obvious. Chimpanzees and crows do not make axes, irrigation channels, fishing nets, windmills, or smartphones.

Recently, psychologists have begun to study the development of this knack for inventing and 'making tools. Granted human achievements in this domain, we might expect our talents to be evident in early childhood. Borrowing from research on crows, researchers have set young children the task of extracting an attractive but difficult-to-access reward: a sticker in a small bucket at the bottom of plexiglass tube – too narrow for children to put their hand in and get hold of the handle to the bucket. Children are provided with suitable materials for solving the problem, notably, a pliable pipe cleaner, as well as unsuitable distractors, such as a piece of string, and encouraged to retrieve the sticker in whatever way they see fit. Granted the prowess of crows on this task, we might reasonably expect young children to also succeed – to take the pipe cleaner rather than the string, form a hook at one end, insert that hooked end into the plexiglass tube, and retrieve the bucket together with its sticker.

Results from various studies show that this expectation is wrong. Beck et al. (2011) found that fewer than 10 percent of three- to five-year-olds and fewer than 50 percent of five- to seven-year-olds figured out that the pipe cleaner could be bent to make a suitable hook. Even among older children (aged seven to eleven years), success was not universal, with approximately one-third failing to make a hook. But children were fast learners or at least gifted copiers. If the experimenter showed them how to bend a pipe cleaner into a hook, most of the children realized that they could also make a hook and then use it to lift the bucket out of the tube, even though this specific use of a hook had not been demonstrated to them. By implication, children realized that a hook would be suitable tool but, for whatever reason, it was only when they were shown a hook that they thought to manufacture one and use it.

We might plausibly speculate that such lack of inventiveness is exacerbated by living in a Western, industrialized world. After all, in that world, children may rarely face a situation in which there is a practical challenge that can only be solved by fashioning a suitable tool. They are surrounded by a plethora of already manufactured tools, from spoons to scissors to iPads. In such a technologically rich environment, there is rarely any need to be inventive. With this in mind, Nielsen et al. (2014) compared the performance of predominantly middle-class three- to five-year-old children in Australia with children from five impoverished Bushman communities in Africa. The Bushman children have little access to prefabricated toys and are prone to make their own from abandoned artifacts. Accordingly, Nielsen and his colleagues speculated that they might be more innovative in toolmaking than Westernized children. However, only 11 percent of Brisbane children and no Bushman children spontaneously made a hook with no prompting by an adult. Echoing the findings of Beck and her colleagues (2011), many children made a hook after being shown how.

Lew-Levy et al. (2021) speculated that children might do poorly on the hook task because of their lack of familiarity with the material supplied for making a hook, notably a pipe cleaner. To evaluate this speculation, they tested BaYaka children in two remote villages in the Likouala region of the Republic of Congo. In one of the two villages, each child was given several pipe cleaners over a two-week period. Children were not instructed what to do with them, but subsequent observation confirmed that the pipe cleaners were often bent and put to use as headbands, armbands, bracelets, necklaces, or hair decoration. Few were found in an unmodified state. By implication, children had had an opportunity to become familiar with the pliability of the pipe cleaners, even if they mostly used them for ornamental rather than practical purposes. In the second village, no pipe cleaners were distributed, and so most children encountered them for the first time when – like the children from the first village – they were presented with a standard version of the hook task (i.e., an opportunity to retrieve an attractive reward, a familiar type of candy, placed in a wicker basket at the bottom of a 20 cm clear tube). Contrary to expectation, children from both villages performed poorly. Only one child (out of sixty-two) from the first village and only two children (out of fifty-six) from the second village successfully formed and used a hook to retrieve the candy. Thus, the opportunity to play with and explore pipe cleaners did not boost children's tool innovation.

One other feature of this study is worth noting. Although there were schools in each of the two villages, children were not regularly in session, and when they were, lessons were delivered for only one or two hours per day. By implication, the children had probably experienced less time in school than the Bushman children tested by Nielsen et al. (2014) and the UK children tested by Beck et al. (2011). Yet, there was no indication that such minimal schooling had boosted their creativity.

In another cross-cultural study, Nelder et al. (2019) studied a somewhat different tool innovation task among five different groups of children: predominantly middle-class children in Brisbane, Australia, and four groups of children living in more traditional or impoverished settings in Vanuata and South Africa. The children were given three different tasks, all involving a sticker located in the middle of a plexiglass tube. In each case, they could poke the sticker out of the tube if they made a suitable rod-like tool, whether by joining shorter pieces together, by removing unnecessary "branches" from a rod of the correct length, or by straightening a thick, curved wire. Echoing past findings, performance on all three tasks improved markedly with age and also improved following a partial demonstration of how to fashion the tool. Moreover, at all ages, the Brisbane children did better than the other four groups, arguably because of their greater familiarity with manufactured items, including rods and plexiglass tubes.

A similar developmental pattern has emerged on another innovation test (Hanus et al., 2011). Children were shown a peanut at the bottom of a narrow transparent tube, a beaker of water was available nearby. Faced with the challenge of retrieving the peanut from the tube, no four-year-old thought of pouring water from the beaker to lift the peanut. Performance was slightly better if the tube was already partially filled with water, so that the peanut was floating part way up the tube. Still, even with this helpful cue, only 17 percent of four-year-olds realized that they could add more water. Eight-year-olds performed better, with 40 percent succeeding on the empty tube and 75 percent on the partially filled tube. As in the hook task, a demonstration proved very helpful for young children. Although few four-year-olds (14 percent) poured water from a bottle into a tube to retrieve a plastic monkey, 61 percent of the unsuccessful children realized what to do once an adult had poured some water into the tube, thereby lifting the monkey part way (Nielsen, 2013).

Taken together, these various studies show that children's performance on simple tasks of tool innovation varies sharply with age. At four years, children mostly fail, whereas by seven or eight years, they are likely to succeed. But beyond such age changes, how far does personality play a role? Noting the fact that children between five and eight years show a relatively mixed performance on the hook task, Beck and her colleagues (2016) asked if personality measures would help identify those who succeed and those who fail. More specifically, children were given a test of executive function as well as divergent thinking. On the face of it, solving a task like the hook task would seem to call for such abilities – for example, an executive ability to inhibit the impulse to reach into the narrow tube and to concentrate instead of finding a more effective solution plus the ability to think of an alternative use for a pipe cleaner. However, no relation was found between these personality measures and performance on the tube task. Indeed, it is important to note that, at this point, there is no good evidence that such a thing as tool innovation ability exists among young children, at least when viewed as a stable individual difference. For example, we do not know if children who solve the hook task would also be likely to solve the floating peanut task. We only know, at this point, that there is typically a marked developmental improvement on both tasks between four and eight years.

That raises the interesting question of why there is a developmental change. What is it about the older as compared to younger children that helps them do better on each task? Given that even younger children perform well when given a simple demonstration, we can rule out certain possibilities. First, it is unlikely that motor skill is the obstacle for younger children. If it were, they would still be likely to fail after a demonstration. Second, it is unlikely that younger children fail to appreciate the usefulness of the techniques demonstrated by the experimenter. Once demonstrated, they readily put those techniques to good use to solve the problem. A more plausible explanation is that younger children are less effective than older children at generating – in their imagination – a suitable technique such as hooking or pouring for the problem in question. That generative ability is likely tied to everyday experience in the sense that older children will have had more exposure to situations in which an object is held or lifted up by means of a hook. Similarly, older children will have had more opportunities to experience situations in which floating objects rise as the liquid level rises, whether it is a toy boat in a bucket, tea leaves in a cup, or a sponge in the sink. In short, on this experience-based account, the main difference between younger and older children is not their inventive ability but their exposure to comparable experiences.

Preliminary support for this speculation is provided by Lew-Levy and colleagues. Alongside the BaYaka children, Lew-Levy et al. (2021) also tested a considerable number of Bondongo children. These children were also given pipe cleaners, which they also put to decorative rather than practical uses. Nevertheless, they were a little more successful at hookmaking than the BaYaka children (even though the majority still failed). A plausible explanation is that, although both groups engage in fishing, they do so differently: Dam fishing is practiced by the BaYaka, but hook fishing is practiced by the Bondongo. Admittedly, fishing hooks are not used to lift wicker baskets containing candy, but they are used to hoist fish out of the water. By implication, the Bondongo were more likely to bring to mind the need for a lifting tool when faced with the hook task. In future research, it will be informative to compare two groups of children – those who are and not familiarized with an artifact of a given type, for example, a hook or a necklace, to assess whether familiarity promotes innovation by cueing the retrieval of a mental template of the type of artifact needed for given context, a template that then guides children's solution efforts.

8.2 Greater Flexibility in Younger Children?

In some ways, the greater inventiveness of older children, documented in the previous section, is surprising. We might expect older children, given their greater experience of how the world typically works, to be less flexible – more stuck in their ways – than younger children. Indeed, when it comes to learning about causation, there is evidence that young children can be more willing to entertain novel hypotheses than older children (Gopnik et al., 2015; Lucas et al., 2014; Seiver et al., 2013). More directly relevant to children's inventiveness, there is also evidence that younger children are quicker to put a familiar tool or artifact to a new use. Building on classic work conducted with adults on so-called functional fixedness (Duncker, 1945) – notably, the tendency to persist with a previously successful strategy even when changing circumstances call for flexibility – German and Defeyter (2000) presented five-, six-, and seven-year-olds with a mix of objects (e.g., a ball, blocks, a magnet, an open-topped box, a pencil, etc.) and asked if they could help Bobo the bear retrieve his toy from a high shelf using any of the objects. Most children came up with a solution, namely, to invert the open-topped box so that it could serve as a kind of platform, to stack up the blocks on that platform, and then have Bobo mount the blocks. Moreover, consistent with the age changes described in the previous section, older children were quicker to arrive at this solution than younger children. Nevertheless, in a parallel condition, the objects were presented inside the open-topped box rather than beside it. In this condition, older children were much slower to arrive at the solution – indeed they were slower than younger children. A plausible explanation for this finding is that older children were displaying functional fixedness. They were prone to view the box as a container if it was presented to them as such – with the toys positioned inside it – and that hampered them in realizing that, despite its usual function, it could be inverted and put to use as a platform.

In a follow-up study with five-, six-, and seven-year-olds, Defeyter and German (2003) obtained similar results with a new set of materials. Children were invited to retrieve a toy animal lodged inside a Perspex tube. Various objects were at their disposal, including either a pencil or a straw that was long enough to poke inside the tube so as to dislodge the animal. In a baseline condition, in which the customary function of these objects was not signaled – the objects were simply placed on the table, along with other distracter objects – most children solved the problem, irrespective of age, and did so within a few seconds. By contrast, younger children outperformed older children in an experimental condition, in which children were reminded of the customary function of the objects before they attempted to retrieve the toy. Thus, the experimenter wrote on a pad with the pencil and returned it to the pad's pencil holder or drank with the straw and left it upright in the cup. In the wake of these reminders, the performance of the six- and seven-year-olds children suffered. Less than half selected the pencil or the straw when making their initial attempt to dislodge the toy and they were considerably slower to start using it. By contrast, the performance of the youngest children – five-year-olds – was barely affected. The majority (60 percent) initially chose the pencil or the straw and typically started to use it within five seconds. In sum, across two studies, older children were susceptible to functional fixedness. Having been given reminders of the standard use for an object, they were less adroit at switching to a nonstandard use. Five-year-olds, by contrast, remained flexible despite such reminders.

However, even five-year-olds know what pencils and straws are used for. So, it is reasonable to ask why were they not also prone to functional fixedness like the older children. Defeyter and German (2003) propose that five-year-olds, unlike older children, are less likely to adopt a "design stance" – to think about an artifact primarily in terms of what it is designed for. More specifically, they argue that when older children are primed by the demonstration of an artifact's standard function, their tendency to adopt the design stance blocks the availability of other potential functions for the artifact. By contrast, when younger children are primed, they regard that function as just one possible function that the artifact can serve, not as its core property. This proposal implies that even when younger and older children have received an equivalent exposure to how an artifact is used, older children, given their adoption of the design stance, will end up displaying greater functional fixedness – less flexibility in repurposing the artifact.

To test this prediction, children in an experimental condition were introduced to two novel artifacts and their uses. One was a Perspex stick fitted with magnets such that when it was dipped into glass holder, several LEDs lit up. The other was a white stick which, when pushed through a hole in a plastic box, activated a high-toned buzzer inside the box. Children were told that Zig, a puppet about to embark on a voyage in space, would use the Perspex stick to make light and the white stick to make music. Children were then presented with the same problem as before, namely, to dislodge a toy animal from a Perspex tube, and a selection of objects that they were free to use. The sticks were presented in their associated receptacles (i.e., the Perspex stick was presented in the glass holder and the white stick in the plastic box). Thus, children in the experimental condition learned about the canonical function of each stick and were reminded of that function by the spatial arrangement of the objects. By contrast, children in a baseline condition were not given a demonstration of the stick functions and the sticks were placed on the table surface rather than in an associated receptacle.

In the baseline condition, most children initially selected the relevant stick although five-year-olds were somewhat slower to do so than six- and seven-year-olds. However, a very different pattern emerged for the experimental condition. Again, the majority of five-year-olds initially selected the relevant stick, and they were no slower than in the baseline condition. By contrast, only a minority of six- and seven-year-olds initially selected the relevant stick, and they were considerably slower than in the baseline condition. Thus, the six- and seven-year-olds again displayed clear signs of functional fixedness – a difficulty in repurposing an artifact if an alternative canonical function had been made salient. These findings lend support to the proposal made by Defeyter and German (2003). Given their design stance, older children are less flexible than younger children – even when each has been familiarized with the function of an artifact to the same extent.

Do these findings attest to the greater creativity of younger children – contrary to the thrust of the findings described in Section 8.1? First, it is important to note that older children displayed greater inflexibility only under certain restricted conditions – notably when the affordances in the immediate environment were arranged to remind them of an artifact's standard purpose. Without such reminders, older children were as flexible as and indeed somewhat quicker than younger children in repurposing an artifact, just as we might expect. That said, it does appear that the design stance can handicap older children – at least when they are reminded of an artifact's standard purpose. But we can ask if that handicap is pervasive or, alternatively, if it is better seen as a small and occasional price to pay for an otherwise beneficial stance. Given the utility of the design stance, the latter conclusion seems appropriate. Children live in a world where most artifacts have a dedicated use: straws are typically used for sucking liquid not for dislodging objects stuck in tube. More generally, the innovative use of artifacts comes in two varieties. On the one hand, there is the challenge associated with generating the mental template for a suitable artifact (e.g., generating the mental template for a hook). On the other hand, there is the challenge associated with repurposing a familiar artifact (e.g., repurposing a box to serve as platform). Overall, the evidence indicates that children get better at generating appropriate artifact templates even if that sometimes leads to hesitation when repurposing is called for.

8.3 Children's Drawings

To further understand children's creativity, it is informative to look at the development of another skill that is characteristically human – drawing (Saito et al., 2014). Parents and teachers generally appreciate the drawings and paintings produced by young children. Selected masterpieces are put on display, or preserved in a folder for posterity. But how imaginative are these works of art? To the extent that children are typically able to draw whatever they want, their drawings would seem to offer a window into what goes on in their imagination. Moreover, unlike the cave art of our ancestors, we can probe children's authorial intentions. We can ask them what they aimed to represent. In his TED talk, mentioned earlier, Robinson recounts the memorable anecdote of a girl who was asked what she was drawing. She explained that she was drawing a picture of God. In reply to the concern that nobody knows what God looks like, she confidently asserted that they soon would – once her drawing was finished.

In gauging the creativity that young children show in their drawings, we can evaluate their representational or graphic skills. However, in thinking about children's imagination and the extent to which it is revealed in their drawings, a more pertinent question concerns what it is that they choose to draw in the first place. It is noteworthy that children's drawings are mostly figurative representations of real entities. They seek to draw someone or something: their mother, a tree, a house, a horse, and so forth. Admittedly, their drawings may not represent the target with much verisimilitude. Men may be depicted as tadpoles and horses as having four legs in a row. But these departures from reality are prompted by young children's limited skill at representation rather than a deliberate effort to go beyond the depiction of reality.

One possible interpretation of the early bias toward the figurative is that children are surrounded by that particular art form. They are rarely exposed to nonfigurative art, certainly in a storybook or on a classroom wall. So, they might conclude that pictures are for the depiction of reality and constrain their own art accordingly. A different possibility is that when children draw on their imagination in order to produce a drawing, they tend to draw on stored representations of reality and not on fantastic departures from reality that they might conjure up in their mind's eye and then transpose onto the page. Karmiloff-Smith (1990) reported findings that are relevant to this issue. She invited children ranging from four to eleven years to produce some ordinary, figurative drawings – to draw a house, a man, and an animal but also to produce drawings much less tied to reality, notably a drawing of house, man, or animal "that does not exist – that nobody has ever seen." Older children aged eight to ten years responded well to this invitation. For example, in drawing a nonexistent man, they often inserted extra elements (e.g., depicted a man with two heads), transposed elements (e.g., depicted a man whose right arm and right leg had been transposed), or imported elements from another category (e.g., depicted a man's head on a horse's body to create a centaur-like fusion). Young children aged four to six years rarely displayed any of these techniques – they resorted to more modest departures from figurative realism, such as alterations of shape or size (e.g., depicting a circular hand) or the omission of an element (e.g., depicting a man with one leg).

Karmiloff-Smith (1990) argued that the limitations of the younger children could be attributed to the inflexibility of their drawing routines – their inability, for example, to add a new element, such as a second head, into their well-rehearsed routine for depicting a human figure. However, subsequent findings indicated that younger children's limitations should be attributed to their difficulties at the initial, generative stage of imagining a nonexistent entity, such as a man with two heads, not at the subsequent drawing execution stage. Thus, when younger children were given external scaffolding at the initial stage in the form of either a verbal prompt ("Do you know how a drawing of a man who doesn't exist could be done? It could be done with two heads.") or a visual prompt (a picture or clay model of a woman with two heads), the majority succeeded in drawing an impossible man, confirming their lack of difficulty at the execution stage (Berti & Freeman, 1997; Zhi et al., 1997) but underlining their difficulty at the earlier generative stage of autonomously imagining what they should draw.

8.4 Creativity in Young Children: Conclusions

In everyday parlance, when we speak of the imagination, we are apt to think of it as a personality trait, a capacity for generating creative ideas and solutions. Indeed, a long tradition of research in psychology has focused on individuals who are especially imaginative or creative in an effort to better understand the conditions leading to their success (Bornstein, 2022). In this final section, I have deliberately approached the imagination with a different perspective. Rather than zooming in on unusual individuals with a record of creative accomplishments, I have instead focused on what might be described as a natural history of the imagination, asking how it develops and what functions it serves in any typically developing child. Indeed, I would argue that, although we have useful psychological measures of individual differences among children in various aspects of their cognitive performance, such as the size of their vocabulary, their numerical skills, and their executive function abilities, we have no widely accepted measures of individual differences in imaginative ability.

When we examine two notable aspects of human creativity – the creation of tools and of visual art – the evidence in both domains strongly suggests that children become more creative and inventive as they get older. Contrary to the popular idea that the creativity of older children is dulled by schooling, older children tend to outperform their less-schooled juniors. In addition, there is no evidence that children with minimal or intermittent schooling are more inventive than children exposed to regular schooling. Nevertheless, despite the robust evidence for improvements with age, it is important to underline one major talent that is evident among younger and older children alike: Their imagination is easily inspired by appropriate guidance and example. Shown how to fashion a hook from a pipe cleaner, they readily make one themselves and put it to practical use. Presented with a description or a depiction of a person with two heads, they can draw their own picture of a man with two heads. In summary, despite their limited creativity when left to their own devices, young children are receptive pupils.

9 Overview

Surveying the arc of research on children's imagination over the last 100 years, we see a shift in conceptualization. Two of psychology's founding fathers, Piaget and Freud, are rarely bracketed together, given their distinctive focus – on cognition in the case of Piaget and on emotion in the case of Freud. Nevertheless, they concurred in their tendency to devalue the imagination and its developmental destiny. In his early writings, Piaget opposed what he called fantasy and free association, hallmarks of early cognition, to objectivity and rationality, hallmarks of the child's emerging logicality (Harris, 1997). For his part, Freud was inclined to see the child's early fantasy life as unruly, as driven hither and thither by unrealizable desires. Ego-driven, rational thought was expected to slowly tame such irrationality. Simply stated, Piaget and Freud tended to characterize children's imagination and fantasy life as indices of primitive, nonrational modes, ill-suited to a sober appraisal of reality.

In the course of the twentieth century, this negative portrait of the child's early imaginative life has steadily given way to a more benign and optimistic conceptualization. Young children are seen as enjoying a special gift: Their tendency to engage in pretend play, to invent imaginary companions, and to create make-believe worlds is seen as a precious endowment, one that gray reality, in the form of unimaginative schooling and rote learning, threatens to suppress or undermine. This characterization of the imagination leads investigators to emphasize the protection or nurturance of pretend play and imagination for fear that the child's healthy development and later creativity will be thwarted (Gray, 2011). Within educational circles, there are pleas that plenty of time for free play be preserved in early education settings, rather than given over to the pressures of a more academic curriculum. Play is promoted as a child-friendly way to foster cognitive skills that are likely to be needed for that academic curriculum (Hirsh-Pasek et al., 2009). This educational perspective is often grounded in theorizing by Vygotsky who argued that play, whether it is pretend play involving props or a game with rules, "continually creates demands on the child to act against immediate impulse" (Vygotsky, 1978, p. 99). From this perspective, it is plausible to expect that the exercise of the imagination will promote children's executive control – their ability to adjust to changing requirements and suppress impulsive desires and responses. Alongside this emphasis on the benefits of play, there is often the hope or expectation that measures of early fantasy and pretending are harbingers of later creativity, despite the lack of any solid evidence for such continuity. Overall, these various ideas signal a shift to what we might call a Romantic conception of the child's imagination, an embrace of the Wordsworthian notion that early childhood is a special time, one that should be protected before "shades of the prison house begin to close upon the growing boy."

I have tried to lay out a third perspective, neither negative nor Romantic. On the one hand, young children do devote, in all manner of cultures, a good deal of time to play, and more specifically to pretend play. But, as argued in Section 1, scrutiny of children's pretend play underscores the fact that the make-believe world that children create and enact in the course of their pretend play is a close cousin of the world that surrounds them, especially with respect to the various practical and workaday activities that they see adults engaged in. Moreover, especially when engaged with a play partner, it is evident that children invest in the pretend world that they cocreate, a host of familiar, causal regularities. In that pretend world, as in the real world, an invisible, make-believe liquid will tip out of an inverted container, wet a surface below, and need to be mopped up with a cloth or tissue. Likewise, as discussed in Section 3, when young children engage in role-play, the various individuals whose parts they enact typically display the familiar psychological attributes of real people: They are agents who can see and hear, experience fear and comfort, have sensations of cold and hunger, think and make plans, and so forth. In short, children transport their limited but useful grasp of basic physics, biology, and psychology into the make-believe worlds that they entertain. Magical or counterintuitive episodes may sometimes make an appearance in children's pretend play, and even in their eyewitness reports, but such fantastical elements tend to have their origin in ideas that adults supply children with. They are not the routine products of the child's independent imagination.

The degree to which children's imaginative life is inspired by their encounters with everyday reality was an important component of Vygotsky's analysis of the imagination. Prior to his justly famous and influential essay on the role of play in development, Vygotsky set out a longer statement on children's imagination and creativity, arguing that the products of the child's imagination are typically grounded in encounters with reality. Indeed, echoing the analysis offered by the French psychologist, Ribot, he concludes that: "if we want to build a relatively strong foundation for a child's creativity, what we must do is broaden the experience we provide him with. All else being equal, the more a child sees, hears, and experiences, the more he knows and assimilates, the more elements of reality he will have in his experience, and the more productive will be the operation of his imagination" (Vygotsky, 2004, p. 15). On this view, it is the experience of reality that provides food for the imagination and enlarges its scope rather than the exotic or misleading ideas that adults are prone to offer.

Granted that the child's imagination is primarily grounded in the recurrent patterns of the real world, it is a powerful device for contemplating real-world possibilities, notably those that might unfold in the future, and well as those that could have happened in the past. Hence, as discussed in Sections 4 and 5, children are increasingly able to figure out what is likely to happen and plan accordingly and to look back at counterfactual possibilities, and derive the relevant causal, deontic, and emotional implications. In addition, via thought experiments, they can discover hitherto unacknowledged truths.

This reality-oriented portrait of the child's imagination is consistent with a great deal of ethnographic and psychological evidence. Still, the notion of a clear-eyed realist is overdrawn in one important domain. As reviewed in Section 6, in the wake of others' testimony, children readily believe in the reality of beings that do not exist, for example, the Tooth Fairy or Santa Claus, and such ideas infuse their perception of reality. Similarly, and again in the wake of others' testimony, many children come to believe in the reality of religious beings and religious phenomena whose existence is debatable or unproven – for example, God, the soul, and Heaven. Indeed, in the latter case, children are likely to retain beliefs formed in childhood well into adulthood. Accordingly, an important challenge for the realist account of the imagination that I have proposed is that it offers no systematic explanation for the fact that children eventually discard their beliefs in some special beings but retain their belief in others.

A comprehensive psychological account of the imagination, including one with a realist emphasis, must also account for its powerful absorptive capacity, and its ability to pull children and adults away from their real-world concerns, sometimes for sustained periods. The developmental approach adopted in Section 7 highlights three aspects of that capacity. First, even in toddlerhood, children can, as indexed by their pretend play, imagine life as another person. That early, role-playing capacity means that young children can readily live in their imagination alongside a story protagonist, viewing the fictive world much he or she does. Second, when adopting that alternative perspective, children become emotionally engaged by the concerns and challenges facing the protagonist. Third, such emotional engagement need not imply any confusion between what is real and what is fictional, especially since we see the same type of emotional engagement among adults.

Finally, with respect to two types of human creativity – toolmaking and art – there are impressive changes with age. Young children have difficulty in spontaneously generating the mental template for a simple tool, such as a hook, or in spontaneously generating the mental template for a drawing of something that does not exist, such as a person with two heads. In each case, older children do better. Contrary to the Romantic vision of early childhood, age generally enhances rather than diminishes children's creativity.

References

Atance, C. M. (2015). Young children's thinking about the future. *Child Development Perspectives*, *9*(3), 178–182. https://doi.org/10.1111/cdep.12128

Bascandziev, I. (in press). Representational pluralism in the service of learning: The case of thought experiments. In M. Bélanger, P. Potvin, S. Horst, S. Shtulman, & E. Mortimer (Eds.), *Representational pluralism*. Routledge.

Bascandziev, I., & Carey, S. (2021). Thought experiments as a means to overcome naive theories in early childhood. *Paper in preparation*.

Bascandziev, I., & Harris, P. L. (2010). The role of testimony in young children's solution of a gravity-driven invisible displacement task. *Cognitive Development*, *25*(3), 233–246. https://doi.org/10.1016/j.cogdev.2010.06.002

Bascandziev, I., & Harris, P. L. (2020). Can children benefit from thought experiments? In A. Levy & P. Godfrey-Smith (Eds.), *The scientific imagination: Philosophical and psychological perspectives* (pp. 262–279). Oxford University Press.

Bascandziev, I., Powell, L., Harris, P. L., & Carey, S. (2016). A role for executive functions in explanatory understanding of the physical world. *Cognitive Development*, *39*(July–September), 71–85. https://doi.org/10.1016/j.cogdev.2016.04.001

Beck, S. R., Apperly, I. A., Chappell, J., Guthrie, C., & Cutting, N. (2011). Making tools isn't child's play. *Cognition*, *119*(2), 301–306. https://doi.org/10.1016/j.cognition.2011.01.003

Beck, S. R., Williams, C., Cutting, N., Apperly, I. A., & Chappell, J. (2016). Individual differences in children's innovative problem-solving are not predicted by divergent thinking or executive functions. *Philosophical Transactions of the Royal Society B: Biological Sciences*, *371*(1690). https://doi.org/10.1098/rstb.2015.0190

Bering, J. M., & Parker, B. D. (2006). Children's attributions of intentions to an invisible agent. *Developmental Psychology*, *42*(2), 253–262. https://doi.org/10.1037/0012-1649.42.2.253

Berti, A. E., & Freeman, N. H. (1997). Representational change in resources for pictorial innovation: A three-component analysis. *Cognitive Development*, *12*(4), 405–426. https://doi.org/10.1016/S0885-2014(97)90020-4

Bettelheim, B. (1991). *The uses of enchantment: The meaning and importance of fairy tales*. Penguin Books. (Original work published 1975.)

Black, J. B., Turner, T. J., & Bower, G. H. (1979). Point of view in narrative comprehension, memory and production. *Journal of Verbal Learning and Verbal Behavior*, *18*(2), 187–198. https://doi.org/10.1016/S0022-5371(79)90118-X

Bornstein, M. H. (2007). On the significance of social relationships in the development of children's earliest symbolic play: An ecological perspective. In A. Göncü & S. Gaskins (Eds.), *Play and development: Evolutionary, sociocultural and functional perspectives* (pp. 101–129). Lawrence Erlbaum Associates.

Bornstein, M. H. (2022). Creativity across the lifespan. In S. W. Russ, J. D. Hoffmann, & J. C. Kaufman (Eds.), *The Cambridge handbook of lifespan development of creativity* (pp. 56–98). Cambridge University Press.

Bower, G. H., & Morrow, D. G. (1990). Mental models in narrative comprehension. *Science*, *247*(4938), 44–48. https://doi.org/10.1126/science.2403694

Boyette, A. H. (2016). Children's play and culture learning in an egalitarian foraging society. *Child Development*, *87*(3), 759–769. https://doi.org/10.1111/cdev.12496

Bryant, D. J., Tversky, B., & Franklin, N. (1992). Internal and external spatial frameworks for representing described scenes. *Journal of Memory and Language*, *31*(1), 74–98. https://doi.org/10.1016/0749-596X(92)90006-J

Busby, J., & Suddendorf, T. (2005). Recalling yesterday and predicting tomorrow. *Cognitive Development*, *20*(3), 362–372. https://doi.org/10.1016/j.cogdev.2005.05.002

Callaghan, T., Moll, H., Rakoczy, H. et al. (2011). Early social cognition in three cultural contexts. *Monographs of the Society for Research in Child Development*, *76*(2), i–142. www.jstor.org/stable/41261530

Chernyak, N., Leech, K. A., & Rowe, M. L. (2017). Training preschoolers' prospective abilities through conversation about the extended self. *Developmental Psychology*, *53*(4), 652–661. https://doi.org/10.1037/dev0000283

Corriveau, K. H., Chen, E. E., & Harris, P. L. (2015). Judgments about fact and fiction by children from religious and non-religious backgrounds. *Cognitive Science*, *39*(2), 353–382. https://doi.org/10.1111/cogs.12138

Corriveau, K. H., Kim, A. L., Schwalen, C., & Harris, P. L. (2009). Abraham Lincoln and Harry Potter: Children's differentiation between historical and fantasy characters. *Cognition*, *112*(2), 213–225. https://doi.org/10.1016/j.cognition.2009.08.007

Davoodi, T., Corriveau, K. H., & Harris, P. L. (2016). Distinguishing between realistic and fantastical figures in Iran. *Developmental Psychology, 52*(2), 221–231. https://doi.org/10.1037/dev0000079

Defeyter, M. A., & German, T. P. (2003). Acquiring an understanding of design: Evidence from children's insight problem solving. *Cognition, 89*(2), 133–155. https://doi.org/10.1016/S0010-0277(03)00098-2

Duncker, K. (1945). On problem-solving. *Psychological Monographs, 58*(5), i–113. https://doi.org/10.1037/h0093599

Gaskins, S. (2000). Children's daily activities in a Mayan village: A culturally grounded description. *Cross-Cultural Research, 34*(4), 375–389. https://doi.org/10.1177/106939710003400405

German, T. P., & Defeyter, M. A. (2000). Immunity to functional fixedness in young children. *Psychonomic Bulletin and Review, 7*(4), 707–712. https://doi.org/10.3758/BF03213010

Glenberg, A., Meyer, M., & Lindem, A. (1987). Mental models contribute to foregrounding during text comprehension. *Journal of Memory and Language, 26*(1), 68–93. https://doi.org/10.1016/0749-596X(87)90063-5

Goldstein, T. R., & Lerner, M. D. (2018). Dramatic pretend play games uniquely improve emotional control in young children. *Developmental Science, 21*(4), Article e12603. https://doi.org/10.1111/desc.12603

Gopnik, A., Griffiths, T. L., & Lucas, C. G. (2015). When young learners can be better (or at least more open-minded) than older ones. *Current Directions in Psychological Science, 24*(2), 87–92. https://doi.org/10.1177/0963721414556653

Gosso, Y., Morais, M. L. S., & Otta, E. (2007). Pretend play of Brazilian children: A window into different cultural worlds. *Journal of Cross-Cultural Psychology, 39*(5), 538–558. https://doi.org/10.1177/0022022107305237

Gray, P. (2011). The decline of play and the rise of psychopathology in children and adolescents. *American Journal of Play, 3*(4), 443–463.

Green, M. C., Brock, T. C., & Kaufman, G. F. (2004). Understanding media enjoyment: The role of transportation into narrative worlds. *Communication Theory, 14*(4), 311–327. https://doi.org/10.1111/j.1468-2885.2004.tb00317.x

Grenell, A., Prager, E. O., Schaefer, C. et al. (2019). Individual differences in the effectiveness of self-distancing for young children's emotion regulation. *British Journal of Developmental Psychology, 37*(1), 84–100. https://doi.org/10.1111/bjdp.12259

Hanus, D., Mendes, N., Tennie, C., & Call, J. (2011). Comparing the performances of apes (Gorilla gorilla, Pan troglodytes, Pongo pygmaeus) and human children (Homo sapiens) in the floating peanut task. *Plos One*, *6*(6). https://doi.org/10.1371/journal.pone.0019555

Harris, P. L. (1997). Piaget in Paris: From "Autism" to logic. *Human Development*, *40*(2), 109–123. https://doi.org/10.1159/000278711

Harris, P. L. (1998). Fictional absorption: Emotional responses to make-believe. In S. Bråten (Ed.), *Intersubjective communication and emotion in early ontogeny* (pp. 336–353). Cambridge University Press.

Harris, P. L. (2000). *The work of the imagination*. Blackwell.

Harris, P. L. (2005). Conversation, pretense, and theory of mind. In J. W. Astington & J. Baird (Eds.), *Why language matters for theory of mind* (pp. 70–83). Oxford University Press.

Harris, P. L. (2009). Piaget on causality: The Whig interpretation of cognitive development. *British Journal of Psychology*, *100*(S1), 229–232. https://doi.org/10.1348/000712609X414222

Harris, P. L. (2012). *Trusting what you're told: How children learn from others*. Belknap Press/Harvard University Press.

Harris, P. L. (2021). Early constraints on the imagination: The realism of young children. *Child Development*, *92*(2), 466–483. https://doi.org/10.1111/cdev.13487

Harris, P. L., Brown, E., Marriott, C., Whittall, S., & Harmer, S. (1991). Monsters, ghosts and witches: Testing the limits of the fantasy-reality distinction in young children. *British Journal of Developmental Psychology*, *9*(1), 105–123. https://doi.org/10.1111/j.2044-835X.1991.tb00865.x

Harris, P. L., German, T., & Mills, P. (1996). Children's use of counterfactual thinking in causal reasoning. *Cognition*, *61*(3), 233–259. https://doi.org/10.1016/S0010-0277(96)00715-9

Harris, P. L., & Jalloul, M. (2013). Running on empty: Observing causal relationships of play and development. *American Journal of Play*, *6*(1), 29–38.

Harris, P. L., & Kavanaugh, R. D. (1993). Young children's understanding of pretense. *Society for Research in Child Development Monographs*, *58*(1), i–107. https://doi.org/10.2307/1166074

Hassabis, D., Kumaran, D., Vann, S. D., & Maguire, E. A. (2007). Patients with hippocampal amnesia cannot imagine new experiences. *PNAS*, *104*(5), 1726–1731. https://doi.org/10.1073pnas.0610561104

Hayne, H., Gross, J., McNamee, S., Fitzgibbon, O., & Tustin, K. (2011). Episodic memory and episodic foresight in 3- and 5-year-old children. *Cognitive Development*, *26*(4), 343–355. https://doi.org/10.1016/j.cogdev.2011.09.006

Hickling, A. K., & Wellman, H. M. (2001). The emergence of children's causal explanations and theories: Evidence from everyday conversation. *Developmental Psychology, 37*(5), 668–683. https://doi.org/10.1037/0012-1649.37.5.668

Hilgard, J. R. (1970). *Personality and hypnosis: A study of imaginative involvement*. University of Chicago Press.

Hirsh-Pasek, K., Golinkoff, R. M., Berk, L. E., & Singer, D. D. (2009). *A mandate for playful learning in the preschool: Presenting the evidence*. Oxford University Press.

Hood, B. (1995). Gravity rules for 2- to 4-year olds. *Cognitive Development, 10*(4), 577–598. https://doi.org/10.1016/0885-2014(95)90027-6

Hood, B. (1998). Gravity does rule for falling events. *Developmental Science, 1*(1), 59–63. https://doi.org/10.1111/1467-7687.00013

Hood, B., Santos, L., & Fieselman, S. (2000). Two-year-olds' naïve predictions for horizontal trajectories. *Developmental Science, 3*(3), 328–332. https://doi.org/10.1111/1467-7687.00127

Huang, I. (1930). Children's explanations of strange phenomena. *Psychologische Forschung, 14*, 63–183. https://doi.org/10.1007/BF00403871

Huang, I. (1943). Children's conception of physical causality: A critical summary. *The Journal of Genetic Psychology, 63*(1), 71–121. https://doi.org/10.1080/08856559.1943.10533231

Joh, A. S., Jaswal, V. K., & Keen, R. (2011). Imagining a way out of the gravity bias: Preschoolers can visualize the solution to a spatial problem. *Child Development, 82*(3), 744–750. https://doi.org/10.1111/j.1467-8624.2011.01584.x

Johnson, C. N., & Harris, P. L. (1994). Magic: Special but not excluded. *British Journal of Developmental Psychology, 12*(1), 35–51. https://doi.org/10.1111/j.2044-835X.1994.tb00617.x

Kalkusch, I., Jaggy, A.-K., Bossi, C. B. et al. (2021). Promoting social pretend play in preschool age: Is providing roleplay material enough? *Early Education and Development, 32*(8), 1136–1152. https://doi.org/10.1080/10409289.2020.1830248

Karmiloff-Smith, A. (1990). Constraints on representational change: Evidence from children's drawings. *Cognition, 34*(1), 57–83. https://doi.org/10.1016/0010-0277(90)90031-E

Kuijpers, M. M., Hakemulder, F., Tan, E. S., & Doicaru, M. M. (2014). Exploring absorbing reading experiences. *Scientific Study of Literature, 4*(1), 89–122.

Lane, J. D. (2020). Probabilistic reasoning in context: Socio-cultural differences in children's and adults' predictions about the fulfillment of prayers and

wishes. *Journal of Cognition and Development, 21*(2), 240–260. https://doi
.org/10.1080/15248372.2019.1709468

Lane, J. D., Ronfard, S. L., Francioli, S. P., & Harris, P. L. (2016). Children's
imagination and belief: Prone to flights of fancy or grounded in reality?
Cognition, 152(July), 127–140. https://doi.org/10.1016/j.cognition.2016
.03.022

Lew-Levy, S., Boyette, A. H., Crittenden, A. N., Hewlett, B. S., &
Lamb, M. (2020). Gender-typed and gender-segregated play among
Tanzanian Hazda and Congolese BaYaka hunter-gatherer children and
adolescents. *Child Development, 91*(4), 1284–1301. https://doi.org/10
.1111/cdev.13306

Lew-Levy, S., Pope, S. M., Haun, D. B. M., Kline, M. A., & Broesch, T. (2021).
Out of the empirical box: A mixed-method study of tool innovation among
Congolese BaYaka forager and Bondong fisher-farmer children. *Journal of
Experimental Child Psychology, 211*, 105223. https://doi.org/10.1016/j
.jecp.2021.105223

Lillard, A. S. (2001). Pretend play as Twin Earth: A social-cognitive analysis.
Developmental Review, 21(4), 495–531.https://doi.org/10.1006/drev
.2001.0532

Lillard, A. S., Lerner, M. D., Hopkins, E. J. et al. (2013). The impact of pretend
play on children's development: A review of the evidence. *Psychological
Bulletin, 139*(1), 1–34. https://doi.org/10.1037/a0029321

Lucas, C. G., Bridgers, S., Griffiths, T. L., & Gopnik, A. (2014). When children
are better (or at least more open-minded) learners than adults: Developmental
differences in learning the forms of causal relationships. *Cognition, 131*(2),
284–199. https://doi.org/10.1016/j.cognition.2013.12.010

McCormack, T., Feeney, A., & Beck, S. R. (2020). Regret and decision-making:
A developmental perspective. *Current Directions in Psychological Science,
29*(4), 346–350. https://doi.org/10.1177/0963721420917688

McCormack, T., O'Connor, E., Cherry, J., Beck, S. R., & Feeney, A. (2019).
Experiencing regret about a choice helps children to delay gratification.
Journal of Experimental Child Psychology, 179, 162–175. https://doi.org/10
.1016/j.jecp.2018.11.005

Mead, M. (1932). An investigation of the thought of primitive children, with
special reference to animism. *Journal of the Royal Anthropological Institute,
62*, 173–190. https://doi.org/10.2307/2843884

Neldner, K., Redshaw, K., Murphy, S. et al. (2019). Creation across cultures:
Children's tool innovation is influenced by cultural and developmental factors. *Developmental Psychology, 55*(4), 877–889. https://doi.org/10.1037/
dev0000672

Nielsen, M. (2013). Young children's imitative and innovative behaviour on the floating object task. *Infant and Child Development, 22*(1), 44–52. https://doi.org/10.1002/icd.1765

Nielsen, M., Tomaselli, K., Mushin, I., & Whiten, A. (2014). Exploring tool innovation: A comparison of Bushman and Western children. *Journal of Experimental Child Psychology, 126,* 384–394. https://doi.org/10.1016/j.jecp.2014.05.008

Nyhout, A., & Ganea, P. A. (2019). Mature counterfactual reasoning in 4- and 5-year-olds. *Cognition, 183,* 57–66. https://doi.org/10.1016/j.cognition.2018.10.027

Orozco-Giraldo, C., & Harris, P. L. (2019). Turning water into wine: Young children's ideas about impossibility. *Journal of Cognition and Culture, 19*(3–4), 219–243. https://doi.org/10.1163/15685373-12340066

Payir, A., & Guttentag, R. (2019). Counterfactual thinking and age differences in judgments of regret and blame. *Journal of Experimental Child Psychology, 183,* 261–275. https://doi.org/10.1016/j.jecp.2019.02.007

Payir, A., Heiphetz, L., Harris, P. L., & Corriveau, K. H. (2022). What could have been done? Counterfactual alternatives to negative outcomes generated by religious and secular children. *Developmental Psychology, 58*(2), 376–391. https://doi.org/10.1037/dev0001294

Payir, A, McLoughlin, N., Cui, Y. K. et al. (2021). Children's ideas about what can really happen: The impact of age and religious background. *Cognitive Science, 45*(10), Article e13054. https://doi.org/10.1111/cogs.13054

Perren, S., Jaggy, A.-K., Kalkusch, I. et al. (2021). Understanding mechanisms underpinning positive impact of pretend play tutoring on social behavior and peer relationships. Paper presented at the Society for Research in Child Development, April 2021.

Piaget, J. (1928). La causalité chez l'enfant. (Children's understanding of causality.) *British Journal of Psychology, 18*(3), 276–301.

Piazza, J., Bering, J. M., & Ingram, G. (2011). "Princess Alice is watching you": Children's belief in an invisible person inhibits cheating. *Journal of Experimental Child Psychology, 109*(3), 311–320. https://doi.org/10.1016/j.jecp.2011.02.003

Prezioso, M. (2022). Absorption in fiction: self-reports of avid and occasional readers. *Paper in preparation.*

Principe, G. F., Kanaya, T., Ceci, S. J., & Singh, M. (2006). Believing is seeing: How rumors can engender false memories in preschoolers. *Psychological Science, 17*(3), 243–248. https://doi.org/10.1111/j.1467-9280.2006.01692.x

Principe, G. F., & Schindewolf, E. (2012). Natural conversations as a source of false memories in children: Implications for the testimony of young witnesses. *Developmental Review, 32*(3), 205–223. http://doi.org/10.1016/j .dr.2012.06.003

Principe, G. F., & Smith, E. (2008a). Seeing things unseen: Fantasy beliefs and false reports. *Journal of Cognition and Development, 9*(1), 89–111. https:// doi.org/10.1080/15248370701836618

Principe, G. F., & Smith, E. (2008b). The tooth, the whole tooth and nothing but the tooth: How belief in the tooth fairy can engender false memories. *Applied Cognitive Psychology, 22*(5), 625–642. https://doi.org/10.1002/acp .1402

Rafetseder, E., Schwitalla, M., & Perner, J. (2013). Counterfactual reasoning from childhood to adulthood. *Journal of Experimental Child Psychology, 114*(3), 389–404. https://doi.org/10.1016/j.jecp.2012.10.010

Rall, J., & Harris, P. L. (2000). In Cinderella's slippers? Story comprehension from the protagonist's point-of-view. *Developmental Psychology, 36*(2), 202–208. https://doi.org/10.1037/0012-1649.36.2.202

Saito, A., Hayashi, M., Takeshita, H., & Matsuzawa, T. (2014). The origin of representational drawing: A comparison of human children and chimpanzees. *Child Development, 85*(6), 2232–2246. https://doi.org/10 .1111/cdev.12319

Seiver, E., Gopnik, A., & Goodman, N. D. (2013). Did she jump because she was the big sister or because the trampoline was safe? Causal inference and the development of social attribution. *Child Development, 84*(2), 443–454. https://doi.org/10.1111/j.1467-8624.2012.01865.x

Shtulman, A. (2009). The development of possibility judgment within and across domains. *Cognitive Development, 24*(3), 293–309. https://doi.org/10 .1016/j.cogdev.2008.12.006

Shtulman, A., & Carey, S. (2007). Improbable or impossible? How children reason about the possibility of extraordinary events. *Child Development, 78* (3), 1015–1032. https://doi.org/pdfdirect/10.1111/j.1467-8624.2007.01047.x

Slade, A. (1987). A longitudinal study of maternal involvement and symbolic play during the toddler period. *Child Development, 58*(2), 367–375. https:// doi.org/10.2307/1130513

Subbotsky, E. V. (1985). Pre-school children's perception of unusual phenomena. *Soviet Psychology, 23*, 91–114.

Subbotsky, E. V. (1994). Early rationality and magical thinking in preschoolers: Space and time. *British Journal of Developmental Psychology, 12*(1), 97–108. https://doi.org/10.1111/j.2044-835X.1994.tb00621.x

Subbotsky, E. V. (2001). Causal explanations of events by children and adults: Can alternative causal modes coexist in one mind? *British Journal of Developmental Psychology, 19* (1), 23–45. https://doi.org/10.1348/026151001165949

Suddendorf, T., & Whiten, A. (2001). Mental evolution and development: Evidence for secondary representation in children, great apes and other animals. *Psychological Bulletin, 127*(5), 629–650. https://doi.org/10.1037/0033-2909.127.5.629

Taylor, M., Carlson, S. M., Maring, B. L., Gerow, L., & Charley, C. M. (2004). The characteristics and correlates of fantasy in school-aged children: Imaginary companions, impersonation and social understanding. *Developmental Psychology, 40*(6), 1173–1187. https://doi.org/10.1037/0012-1649.40.6.1173

Tellegen, A., & Atkinson, G. (1974). Openness to absorbing and self-altering experiences ("absorption"), a trait related to hypnotic susceptibility. *Journal of Abnormal Psychology, 83*(3) 268–277. https://doi.org/10.1037/h0036681

Thibodeau, R. B., Gilpin, A. T., Brown, M. M., & Meyer B. A. (2016). The effects of fantastical pretend-play on the development of executive functions: An intervention study. *Journal of Experimental Child Psychology, 145*(May), 120–138. https://doi.org/10.1016/j.jecp.2016.01.001

Thibodeau, R. B., Turley, D., DeCaro, J. A., Gilpin, A. T., & Nancarrow, A. F. (2020). Physiological substrates of imagination in early childhood. *Social Development, 30*, 867–882. https://doi.org/10.1111/sode.12505

Vaden, V. C., & Woolley, J. D. (2011). Does God make it real? Children's belief in religious stories from the Judeo-Christian tradition. *Child Development, 82*(4), 1120–1135. https://doi.org/10.1111/j.1467-8624.2011.01589.x

Vostrovsky, C. (1895). A study of imaginary companions. *Education, 15*, 383–398.

Vygotsky, L. S. (1978). *Mind in society: The development of higher psychological processes*. Harvard University Press.

Vygotsky, L. S. (2004). Imagination and creativity in childhood. *Journal of Russian and East European Psychology, 42*(1), 7–97. https://doi.org/10.1080/10610405.2004.11059210

Weisberg, D. P., & Beck, S. R. (2012). The development of children's regret and relief. *Cognition and Emotion, 26*(5), 820–835. https://doi.org/10.1080/02699931.2011.621933

White, R. E., & Carlson, S. M. (2016). What would Batman do? Self-distancing improves executive function in young children. *Developmental Science, 19*(3), 419–426. https://doi.org/10.1111/desc.12314

White, R. E., Prager, E. O., Schaefer, C. et al. (2017). The "Batman Effect": Improving perseverance in young children. *Child Development, 88*(5), 1563–1571. https://doi.org/10.1111/cdev.12695

White, R. E., Thibodeau-Nielsen, R. B., Palermo, F., & Mikulski, A. M. (2021). Engagement in social pretend play predicts preschoolers' executive function gains across the school year. *Early Childhood Research Quarterly, 56,* 103–113. https://doi.org/10.1016/jecresq.2021.03.005

Wolf, D. P., Rygh, J., & Altshuler, J. (1984). Agency and experience: Actions and states in play narratives. In I. Bretherton (Ed.), *Symbolic play: The development of social understanding* (pp. 195–217). Academic Press. https://doi.org/10.1016/B978-0-12-132680-7.50011-9

Woolley, J. D., Boerger E. A., & Markman, A. B. (2004). A visit from the Candy Witch: Factors influencing young children's belief in a novel fantastical being. *Developmental Science, 7*(4), 456–468. https://doi.org/10.1111/j.1467-7687.2004.00366.x

Woolley, J. D., & Ghossainy, M. (2013). Revisiting the fantasy-reality distinction: Children as naïve skeptics. *Child Development, 84*(5), 1496–1510. https://doi.org/10.1111/cdev.12081

Zhi, Z., Thomas, G. V., & Robinson, E. J. (1997). Constraints on representational change: Drawing a man with two heads. *British Journal of Developmental Psychology, 15,* 275–290. https://doi.org/10.1111/j.2044-835X.1997.tb00521.x

Ziegler, F. V., & Acquah, D. J. (2013). Stepping into someone else's shoes: Children create spatial mental models from the protagonist's point of view. *European Journal of Developmental Psychology, 10,* 546–562. https://doi.org/10.1080/17405629.2012.744689

Ziegler, F., Mitchell, P., & Currie, G. (2005). How does narrative cue children's perspective-taking? *Developmental Psychology, 41,* 115–123. https://doi.org/10.1037/0012-1649.41.1.115

Cambridge Elements ☰

Child Development

Marc H. Bornstein

Eunice Kennedy Shriver National Institute of Child Health and Human Development,
Bethesda
Institute for Fiscal Studies, London
UNICEF, New York City

Marc H. Bornstein is an Affiliate of the *Eunice Kennedy Shriver* National Institute of Child Health and Human Development, an International Research Fellow at the Institute for Fiscal Studies (London), and UNICEF Senior Advisor for Research for ECD Parenting Programmes. Bornstein is President Emeritus of the Society for Research in Child Development, Editor Emeritus of *Child Development*, and founding Editor of *Parenting: Science and Practice.*

About the Series

Child development is a lively and engaging, yet serious and real-world subject of scientific study that encompasses myriad theories, methods, substantive areas, and applied concerns. Cambridge Elements in Child Development addresses many contemporary topics in child development with unique, comprehensive, and state-of-the-art treatments of principal issues, primary currents of thinking, original perspectives, and empirical contributions to understanding early human development.

Cambridge Elements ≡

Child Development

Printed in the United States
by Baker & Taylor Publisher Services